Once Upon A Tree

CALVIN MILLER

Once Upon A Tree

Answering the Ten Crucial Questions of Life

SIGNATURE SERIES

HOWARD
PUBLISHING CO.

Our purpose at Howard Publishing is to:

- *Increase faith* in the hearts of growing Christians
- *Inspire holiness* in the lives of believers
- *Instill hope* in the hearts of struggling people everywhere

Because He's coming again!

Published by Howard Publishing Co., Inc.
3117 North 7th Street, West Monroe, Louisiana 71291-2227
in association with the literary agency of Alive Communications, Inc.,
7680 Goddard Street, Suite 200, Colorado Springs, Colorado 80920

Edited by Philis Boultinghouse
Interior design by John Luke

Editor's Note: The event of the Cross is central to the entirety of this book. The
word *Cross* is capitalized when referring to the "event" of the Crucifixion. It is lowercased when referring to the wooden object, the "cross" as a symbol of Christianity,
the "cross" the followers of Christ bear. It is capitalized or lowercased according to its
treatment in quoted material.

Contents

Preface

All I am and hope for is riveted to that one mysterious moment when history froze into focus: the Cross of Christ! At that pivot of history, time stood still. Nothing moved. In time, I came upon this place; and I found both excellence and shame.

There Jesus' sacrifice stands embarrassingly close to my self-centeredness. There I bring my greed and beg his generosity. There I bring all my trivial whimperings and marvel again at the depths of his suffering and how far he was willing to go.

Again and again I ask myself what binds his dying to my living. The only answer is love—undeserved and unfailing: I need him. It is as if I open my thin wallet and find it gorged with the treasuries of God. At the Cross, my need meets his generosity. But why should my need be of any concern to God? Why should it forge the very nails that held him to the wood? Looking upward, I realize I am being stalked by God's passionate and illogical love. I cannot lay aside my need for him, and he is incapable of laying aside his love for me.

Did he really die two thousand years ago? It seems not so. It seems he is dying now—ever dying. I daily gaze upon his Cross, and I am rebuked by my own pursuit of ease. I cannot place Good Friday in the distant past. Good Friday is last Friday, next Friday, every Friday. I must daily die to self and live for him. I must count on its continuing glory; I must repeatedly reckon with its demands.

I never find much of a crowd at Calvary. Most of the time, Jesus and I are alone there—just the two of us. The centurion, the Pharisees, the thieves, the bystanders—they all disappear and leave us engrossed in our ongoing conversation. We are host to each other in a dialogue of spirit that makes life possible. At such moments the two of us do not spin out stale philosophies. Rather, we despise them, for we see their lack of substance. In beholding him as he is, I cringe at what I am. But he assures me that even with all my self-will, I remain valuable to God. "Behold my hands," he says, "and you will know how great is your value unto my Father." Dear God! Was there ever love like this! Here is Jesus—my Emmaus love—and I confess that my heart burns within me even as we talk (Luke 24:32).

"Come, Jesus," I say, "let me see your dying etched on my conscience of convenience. Your Cross is not confined to the past. Were those in the crucifixion crowd your only contemporaries? Nonsense! I, too, am your contemporary.

"The Cross is now...now...while I must minister to a

new widow locked in the trauma of grief. While your life ebbs away on your cross, she begs me to give her one good reason for going on with her life. There you hang while all that bloody wood presides quietly over an embittered couple whose bitterness has yet to be crucified. Their marriage will not survive if they refuse to walk out of their dark tomb. It is even now being sealed against them."

All of life is packaged in suffering, and its package is severe. His dying is my treasure, for it shows me the "how and why" of my own dying—and of my living, too. On we talk, hanging side by side, cross to cross. I turn to him and admit that I, too, am crucified (Gal. 2:20). Wise living is possible only when I remember that my death is hurriedly approaching. My days are swifter than a weaver's shuttle (Job 7:6). How honest is the psalmist: "[Lord,] teach us to number our days aright, that we may gain a heart of wisdom" (Ps. 90:12 NIV).

I know my days are precious, because they are few. My cross-to-cross talking with Jesus, therefore, must come not only on Good Fridays, but on Bad Tuesdays as well. Indeed his Cross is my everyday business. And I am glad my days are few, for every sunset tells me life is brief and I must long for a more eternal fellowship. At these rare moments of confronting the brevity of my life, I know a "crossly" brotherhood with Jesus; I glory in the fellowship of his sufferings (Phil. 3:10). For only when the two of us have died together will the both of us live on—past the sunset markers of my tiny years. He has died! My longings shall at last sleep in the security of his resurrection. For my dying Savior has taught me that only his victory over death can save. This is my confidence. God is the manager of my mortality. I may live the dying life in confidence. I know that all my affairs are in good hands. *Father, into thy hands I commend my spirit.*

Introduction

I used to wonder why the week of Jesus' crucifixion takes up so much space in the New Testament (it consumes nearly half of John and from a third to a fourth of the other Gospels), while the earlier thirty-two years and fifty-one weeks of Jesus' life are crowded into the smaller opening chapters of the Gospels. Other writers and thinkers have observed that facing death clears the mind. It allows us the glaring light of focus to fall on all we really believe. At the Cross the critical philosophies of a thirty-three-year-old field-rabbi come under sharp scrutiny. For the three decades of his life, he taught us not to be afraid. Now he is dying! I must test his philosophies. I must study him carefully.

Is he nervous? Is he afraid? I must see if my teacher is able to stand by his teaching. He taught me I would live forever. So I scrutinize the Cross. He is gasping. He is dying. Are there chinks in his confidence? Does it hold? Is he steady and secure before the jeering mob? He taught me always to hold to my faith. So looking at his Cross, I must ask, "Does *he*?" He taught me to be happy in persecution

(Matt. 5:10–12). Now he stands naked in judgment! Does he live out his own demanding beatitude?

The Cross puts the Son of God in our laboratory. There we dump the acid of our skepticism on his claims. All those philosophies he spun out on sweet summer days—will they stand? Can he answer? Will Jesus endure with godly fortitude, or will he whimper, complain, and recant? Will he excoriate his accusers or bless them? Will he turn the other cheek or rage against them in wrath? Will he knock the jeering world to pieces or love it in the midst of its bloody cruelty? Here at Calvary the great God of Scripture passes under the microscope of human proof. The Cross tells all and then asks us to decide whether Jesus really is the way, the truth, and the life (John 14:6).

At the age of sixty-five, I am rapidly moving closer to my own death. As the years speed by, has my view of suffering and dying changed? How do I feel about *his* death as I draw ever closer to *my own*? Nothing has changed in how I feel about his dying. All that is new is the deepening of my passion for its reality. The Cross remains for me the certain triumph of Christ. I see the same things I saw when I was thirty, but I see them ever so much more clearly now. His death and dying are still my best teachers on how I must do it when my time comes. My vision seems clearer even as my eyesight worsens. But Jesus' how-tos of dying are not the only lessons of his Cross. There are other critical lessons at

Calvary. It is to the Cross I turn to deal with my grief, my pain…my meaninglessness.

This planet is a crying place, and I have done my share. I will always need to listen to his Cross. I've never been good at enduring pain. I need his Cross to coach me in this matter, for the idea of living with extended pain terrifies me. Then, too, all of us have wondered just how important we really are. Does this world truly need us? Is there any real meaning in our lives? I have been coached by the Cross of my gracious Lord to confidently look the Medusa of meaninglessness in the face.

As I draw ever closer to life's great finality, I am ready for the Cross's best lessons. Not long ago, my doctor told me I must go to a specialist; and the specialist told me that I would likely have to have a valve replacement in my heart. While I wasn't altogether sure that I would die during that procedure, for the first time in my life I felt the reality of my own death. Friends who knew both the prognosis and my fears prayed for me. Perhaps their prayers were efficacious, and perhaps the early prognosis had been overly hasty—for I was granted a joyous reprieve. The operation was unnecessary.

Still, the uncertainty of those days clarified my vision of all those things I thought I believed. Death was not as terrifying as I had thought it would be. I had not faced any actual pain, yet it seemed somehow bearable ahead of time. From my little vista of dim finality, I could see myself, like Christ, praying "Father, into thy hands..."

Now I know the Cross *does* answer all—all the important questions! Thus in this book I take in hand a look at the fearsome doctrines of our lives. There are ten of them:

- human meaning
- salvation
- grief
- the need for community
- betrayal
- accountability
- death and dying
- self-sacrifice
- pain
- transcendence

One by one, I shall (for my sake and perhaps for yours) open these dark, heavily sealed packages at the Cross and expose them to the light of Jesus' gallant dying. As the beautiful hymn expresses, I know that when that "light of sacred story" falls upon my fears, I will say with Paul, "Truly the sufferings of this present time are not worthy to be compared with the glory that shall be" (Rom. 8:18).

Come with me to the end of Jesus' life; for only there can we understand the important issues of ours.

But when the fulness

of the time was come,

God sent forth his Son…

to redeem them

that were under the law.

Paul of Tarsus

GALATIANS 4:4 KJV

The Nail That Holds All

THE CROSS AND THE ISSUE OF MEANING

"You are a king, then!" said Pilate.

Jesus answered, "You are right in saying I am a king. In fact, for this reason I was born, and for this I came into the world, to testify to the truth. Everyone on the side of truth listens to me."

"What is truth?" Pilate asked. With this he went out again to the Jews and said, "I find no basis for a charge against him."
(John 18:37–38 NIV)

When Pilate asked Jesus, "What is truth?" Christ gave him no verbal answer. Jesus may have remained silent because he realized that Pilate was really asking, "Why am I alive?" It is my number one question. It is your number one question. Only God can answer that question for us. And until we have his answer, our lives themselves remain a question.

This plaintive issue always comes from our deep hunger to know the meaning of life. "Why am I alive?" is every suicide's question. Up to the very moment the lips taste the steel of the cold gun barrel, it remains a desperate question. If the despairing could only find meaning in life, death

7

would never be their choice. Life is only painful when we cannot think of why it was given to us. We are ever baffled over Pilate's question, "What is truth?" Truth, whatever its glory, is not always as near as we would like. Our need for God's answers is often met by a groaning silence. Which of us has not stared into the ashen face of our existence and cried, "Father, who am I? Why am I here?" From time to time, which of us has not wept because we doubted God or sought some evidence that our lives were more than a pointless ache in a cold, uncaring world? We must have both a reason to live and the passion to want to. We find that if we know the *why* of living, we can put up with any *how*.

Pilate must have envied Jesus when he saw that Christ could celebrate his life-purpose on the very brink of death. He must have coveted Jesus' confidence in finding a powerful purpose in his pending execution. Jesus kept quiet not because he did not know the answer to Pilate's question. He kept quiet because silence is the way we talk when all that may be said, has been.

Nailing the Ages Together

Once upon a tree, there was a Savior. And when this Savior quit talking and started dying, the eloquence of God roared forth in thunder. History is nailed together! Literally! The human story, from its beginning to the Cross, was disconnected and void of meaning. Without a verbal explanation, Jesus nailed the ages together and gave them continuity. Ever since that first nail was driven, the world's story makes sense. Since then, there is a vital interrelatedness between its separated chapters. Since then, we who choose to bear his cross can know why we're on this planet. We have stared into the face of confusion, and we have won. There is no *why* question for us. Our lives are God's great *Gloria!* No wonder the apostle tells us, "Speak to one another with psalms, hymns and spiritual songs. Sing and make music in your heart to the Lord" (Eph. 5:19 NIV). So we praise. Praise doesn't *supply* us with answers. Praise *is* the answer. The discordant empty places of our lives now ring with saving symphonies.

WE FIND THAT IF WE KNOW THE *WHY* OF LIVING, WE CAN PUT UP WITH ANY *HOW*.

After Jesus left Pilate, following his trial, he met a hammer man. We will never know this man's name. We do know he was a state employee. Ignorant of his own vital role in things too big for him to imagine, he drove the first nail through the hand of a man and into a cross. He was so completely lost in his bloody business that he took no time to scratch his name upon the wood, so we cannot know him.

But looking back over history, we know that it is mostly the guilty who crucify the innocent. The Cross is but one more example of James Russell Lowell's "truth forever on the scaffold, wrong forever on the throne." Yet, in a more honest sense, we do know this hammer man. Have we not seen him in our dressing-room mirror? Does he not gawk back at us from the glass? It is only when I study the executioner's face and see it as my own that I shed my best, most honest tears. The nails also are mine. The bloody wood too.

But Calvary is not just my giving tree where I give God all I am. God is the real giver there, and I the joyous taker. There I suck from the marrow of divinity the knowledge that I am here by appointment. In seeing the reason Christ came into the world, I know that I, too, am here for a reason. In celebrating all Jesus has done for me, I must not be too hard on the hammer man. Could he really have been expected to understand the significance of the nails he drove? After all, he had spiked four other hands to crosses that dismal morning in spring. Those hands belonged to local hooligans, convicted by the courts of sedition and treason. And as the world sees it, capital crimes do deserve capital punishment.

> THERE I SUCK FROM THE MARROW OF DIVINITY THE KNOWLEDGE THAT I AM HERE BY APPOINTMENT.

So, with the "innocence" of ignorance, he drove the critical nail of history. Blame him little. A hammer man only drives the nails where the state says to drive them. Not even a wise judge can look at a man's hands and pronounce him innocent or guilty. So we should not expect anything more of a menial state employee. He is not at fault. The hands of robbers and carpenters look very much alike; thus, for him, the nail was driven and forgotten.

But not for us.

The Apostolic Recipe for Life

For us a thin and needy light focuses on his cross. Like someone being wakened from a deep sleep, we ask, "What does this mean?" Oddly enough, the first to ask this question were fishermen, revenue collectors, peasants, and prostitutes, who had through his dying become respectable. These were the ones who wrote the Gospels—those all-inclusive biographies of Christ.

It is right that we have trusted their report. In the first century the apostles were the needy who desired to know him. Now we are the needy whose greatest need is to know him. They were the old generation of beggars who packaged the bread of salvation for our generation. We now eat from their recipe of life.

I have asked the Father that I might never forget that these who first wrote of the Cross were my brothers. They called him Lord in centuries gone by that I might call him Lord in mine. They stood at the Cross, drinking of its life.

11

Now they crook their fingers to beckon me to a glorious altar—and there I am reborn. Now I can trade all my little reasons to live for one big one.

Those souls of old had little status. Yet they began to insist very noisily that the eighteenth year of Emperor Tiberius was history's most important—for it was the Year of the Cross. It was God's year for answering our one simple question: "Why am I on this planet?" These followers of the Christ couldn't change their minds about the truth of the Cross, and they wouldn't change the subject. They got loud and stayed loud! They shouted it from dungeon windows and prison stocks. They were buried beneath piles of stones thrown in anger. Their heads rolled. Some were crucified in their defense of the crucifixion. And to what have these martyrs (or "witnesses," for that is what the word *martyr* means) called us? Have they called us to some Sunday, cafeteria-style church where we select the worship we want to hear, then castigate others with different tastes? Have we been summoned to committee quarrels where our prosaic egos lobby for control within Christ's body of believers? God forbid!

These who could not change their minds about the Cross have called us to their own private Calvary and, more important, to ours. Gradually they triumphed! Ever so slowly, as they convinced the world that the central event in time and eternity was the Cross, they bade us look with contempt on our own naive discipleship. Jesus died. Surely, we can apply ourselves to straighten out the cricks in our meaningless, disconnected story. How much we need the ancient hammer man to spike our own short, spastic lives to something more enduring.

It is the Cross's power over my meaningless story that draws me to it. Poets and composers may raise the Cross to the center of art and literature, but only our need and hunger can raise it to the center of our lives.

When I was nine years old, I heard the Cross preached in such a way that I knew I was loved. There my childhood was marked with a sense of awe. The *titulus*—that I.N.R.I. (*Iesus Nazarenus rex Iudaeorum*, John 19:19 VULGATE) sign above the cross—for me read only "Abba." I had a Father, and he had two sons. His only begotten Son purchased meaning and gave it, wrapped in thorns, to me, the son he had so lately adopted (Rom. 8:15).

What's the Use of Living?

We will never see the Cross as the center of our own history until we see it as the center of all history. Other parts of history may seem to have deeper meaning for our existence. We might name the Code of Hammurabi or the Decalogue or the Magna Carta as of equal importance. The year 27 might not be as significant to us as 44 B.C. or 1066 or 1588 or even 1945. Yet none of these events is as fundamental to all meaning as is the Cross. Since we cannot live long on earth, we must hurriedly ask life's vital questions. They are not new. The human race between the Stone Age and our third millennium have been vexed in lonely moments by the same gut-wrenching questions: Where have I come from? Where am I going? What's the use of my being here? The Cross has answered all.

The Cross replies splendidly and clearly to these issues while secular historians poke through their musty old annals in a vain attempt to find the answers. Such history can inform us, but it cannot keep our souls alive.

HIS ANSWERS COULD NOT BE SPOKEN; THEY HAD TO BE SUFFERED.

These more than matter-of-fact questions require more than matter-of-fact replies. I despair, yet I am hungry for hope. I am dying, and yet I want to live. As I face these great question marks, I plead, "O God, give me no words. Give me something that transcends talk. Let me collide with your answers in something as visible as the blood of Yahweh dripping from the steel head of a hammer. Maybe, then, I can actually live." A great ballet artist, on completion of a masterful interpretation, was asked why she performed the dance in her particular way. "If I could have said it, do you suppose I would have danced it?" she replied. So it was with Christ.

He would not have answered us with a cross if he could have written an essay.

His answers could not be spoken; they had to be suffered. This photo of meaning was caught on vivid film and developed over three days in darkness. Men and women argued with themselves as to what his sacrifice meant. With the emergence of that first Easter, man's deepest longings were fulfilled. Their hard questions were silenced by substance.

Our Unimportant Histories

How are these basic questions related to history? How is our personal history related to the Cross? History is more than the progression of events and dates. It is composed of people who get hungry, curse the light, love, weep, and sometimes die in convulsion and pain. So it is correct to say that the Battle of Salamis was fought in 480 B.C. It is correct, but not very adequate.

History comes in three modes. The first is the remote, distant mode. At Salamis, Greek children were snatched from the combat area. Some were killed in the process, and their mothers fell to asking all those vital questions. There were Athenian lads who had never killed a man, trying desperately to find some justification for what they were asked to do. There was crusty old Xerxes, who watched as the smaller Grecian navy outmaneuvered his great Persian fleet. Knowing the pain of failure, all the old questions came to him too.

There is a second mode of history. This history is recent and touches our lives. Iwo Jima is such history for me. I was seven years old when that battle was fought. I lived in a small Oklahoma town. It was history that our little community participated in. We sent the finest, most debonair and handsome young man in our neighborhood to participate in that history. He came back on a hospital ship, twisted, crippled, and spastic. He never married. Certainly those old questions came to him: Where have I been? Why me? Where will I end up? And, of course, history with its muted volumes stands silent.

The third mode of history is our own current immersion in the vast everydayness of life. We are all immersed in this contemporary history. We are living in the Year of the War on Terrorism and Uncertain Economics. We are the post-nine-eleven people. Television's nightly news has brought us an awareness of history as it is being made hour by hour. "One hundred men died in this attack," we hear a commentator say, or "There was heavy fighting in that area" or "It was the greatest air tragedy of the year to date." These facts link our present to the ongoing story of human heartbreak. Still, if these events do not directly involve us, we often stake them at the edge of consciousness and forget them.

We are too busy living out our own personal lives. We are the urban urbane, involved with civic associations to gain status. We are presidents of sports leagues. We work on our "Who's Who" certificates. If one of our lodge brothers doesn't blackball us, we could soon rise to the rank of "Cobra" in the "Royal Order of the Mongoose." Finally, there is that dollar-a-year charity board to which we were elected. If we run fast enough, it could earn us an invitation to the governor's ball.

This is our micro-history! While we love these involvements, there are still times when, like an actor worn out from rehearsal, we wonder if the drama is worth it. Then those plaguing questions of meaning come flying out of the darkness to haunt us. Despite all the energy we have expended, we feel a lack of depth and achievement. We have been busy—no doubt about that—but it is a squirrel-cage frenzy that gets us nowhere.

Trapped by the unimportant kind of history we are making, we have, perhaps, two ways out. There is the aspirin bottle, which will at best only postpone the questions. Or there is the Cross of Christ, which was driven like a wedge into time for the sake of time. It does not simply brush the questions aside; it answers them. It is God's best antidote for our own unsatisfying participation in the human struggle.

The Cross of Righteousness—
The Symbol of Christ's Love

The Cross can answer our conflicts because it, too, is steeped in conflict. For two hundred decades now, cynics have crawled out of every little corner of time to throw rocks at the Cross. Philosophers have pelted it with laughter, only to meet the words of Paul, one of the Cross's greatest defenders: "The preaching of the cross is to them that perish foolishness; but unto us which are saved it is the power of God" (1 Cor. 1:18 KJV).

The logicians have cried that the message of the Cross is too unbelievable for the educated or the wise, but the Cross has answered again: "Where is the wise? where is the scribe? where is the disputer of this world? hath not God made foolish the wisdom of this world?" (1 Cor. 1:20 KJV).

Has the Cross successfully answered its critics? Well, many generations of critics are now gone, and still the Cross remains. It brings us new meaning. It sets our feet on a pathway that leads somewhere important. We want the Cross to do this for the whole world at once, but that is not the way of the Cross. The Cross gains its converts one heart at a time. It enlists its army soldier by soldier.

The Cross will always be there to remind us that we have come from God who made us with the ability to choose, hoping we would be strong enough to choose the right course.

18

But the Cross, too, has come from God. It has come because we who were created good have gone bad. Given the power to choose between sin and righteousness, we chose sin. However, we need not despair over this lack of righteousness in our lives. The Cross offers a firm and mystical logic so that all men and women—all who are captive to sin—may accept its immaculate righteousness and glory in its depth of meaning.

> THE CROSS GAINS ITS CONVERTS ONE HEART AT A TIME. IT ENLISTS ITS ARMY SOLDIER BY SOLDIER.

But what has this tree of execution to do with righteousness in our lives? Everything! Because the man who died there did so only after thirty-three years of perfect existence. Year after year he met each of the ten commandments without a single violation. He was tempted to commit every sin in the thesaurus of human iniquity, yet he never committed one (Heb. 4:15).

The Cross became the symbol of Christ's love of holiness. It was because he clung so tightly to it that he faced the Cross in the first place. Christ could have avoided his death by surrendering his sinlessness. He could have lied his way out of it. When the Roman magistrate asked him if he was a king, he could have said, "Who, me?" and avoided the Cross.

When the priests asked him if he was the Son of God, he could have said, "Why, the very idea is ridiculous!" But to have answered with a lie would have forfeited his holiness. Jesus knew that he was both the Son of God and the King of Jews. Loving both God and the truth, he refused to lie about it. He laid hold of holiness and refused to abandon it, even to save his life.

At Calvary, truth died, holding out its bloody hands to falsehood. So now I, too, have come at the end of a chain of men and women two thousand years long, asking Christ to take the fullness of his righteousness (or holiness) and place it in the center of my life. I have tried to live without sin and have failed. Yet I can still own holiness and live in the happiness it serves. Although I cannot depend on my own righteousness to indwell me, his righteousness is dependable.

> **IF I DARE TO SALUTE THE CROSS, EVEN MOMENTARILY, I MUST SERVE IT HOURLY FOR THE REST OF MY LIFE.**

Is it not time to raise the Cross in the middle of my life? I must be careful before I answer. His Cross will not coexist with my present way of life. I may not raise the Cross as something incidental to my petty social involvements. If I dare to salute it, even momentarily, I must serve it hourly for the rest of my life. The Cross is the supreme example of righteousness and can never belong to the person who will not show it supreme respect.

The crucifixion invites us to complete the cycle of human failure and redemption. Each of us is created by God. But only in the Cross are we recreated by way of Christ's sacrifice to enjoy our fellowship with God. Years ago I wrapped my own search for meaning in these twelve lines.

> *Poor souls, we are without purpose,*
> *From battle to battle defiled.*
> *We are orphans who nervously search*
> *For a Father to call us his child.*
> *Anxiety throbs in our heads;*
> *Our mind tries some purpose to see.*
> *There's a strange, empty vacuum of pain*
> *In the place where our hearts ought to be.*
> *There can yet be life for the lifeless.*
> *The hopeless have one hope sublime;*
> *For our Lover has driven His Cross*
> *In the cascading decades of time.*

The hands of Christ

seem very frail

For they were broken

by a nail.

But only they

reach heaven at last

Whom these frail,

broken hands hold fast.

John R. Moreland

CHAPTER TWO

The Wood of the New Agreement

THE CROSS AND THE ISSUE OF SALVATION

Now it was the day of Preparation, and the next day was to be a
special Sabbath. Because the Jews did not want the bodies left on
the crosses during the Sabbath, they asked Pilate to have the legs
broken and the bodies taken down. The soldiers therefore came
and broke the legs of the first man who had been crucified with
Jesus, and then those of the other. But when they came to Jesus
and found that he was already dead, they did not break his legs.
Instead, one of the soldiers pierced Jesus' side with a spear, bring-
ing a sudden flow of blood and water. (John 19:31–34 NIV)

"We must kick the darkness 'til it bleeds daylight," cried
Bruce Cockburn.[1] Dylan Thomas advised us: "Do not go
gentle into that good night.... Rage, rage against the dying
of the light."[2] More than they knew, perhaps, these poets
sang out God's definition of the Cross and our salvation.
Jesus on Good Friday kicked the darkness till it bled light;
indeed, he raged against the dying of the light until he had
purchased for us the entire realm of light.

Once upon a tree, our Savior bled a royal river of
access, whose rich flood ended in eternity. Drop by drop his

war against sin drove back the forces of hell until every drop was gone. "It is finished," cried the Son, and the angels broke the universal hush with the battle cry of human liberation. His ghastly task finished all and left us with nothing else to do but lower our eyes and whisper *miserere*—have mercy upon us. So I bow my head and bend my knee before this mighty carpenter-conqueror. His place of dying lies at a fork in life's roads. Hell lies down one avenue and heaven up the other; and where the turnpike splits, hangs the Savior who illuminates my choice of destinies. I must stop where these two roads diverge and, like Bunyan's Pilgrim, look up into that faithful, thorn-ringed face. I cannot look too long, for just the shortest glance causes me to cast my eyes downward and beg him answer one question: Is all of this for me?

I'm disturbed that the "why" of Calvary is so untroubling to the masses. If Jesus had been crucified in our day, the press release might have gone something like this:

—United Press International. The United Arab Republic announced by repeated broadcast on Radio Cairo that Jesus Bar Joseph was executed for inciting riots and aiding in insurrection. His repeated inferences that he was some sort of king or leader seemed to be a threat to the national and international stability of many Near Eastern countries. His execution was unprotested even by his closest followers. Officials in Tel Aviv felt that Jesus, who only days earlier had caused a riot in Jerusalem, might have been planning a military coup. Although no specific charge has yet been released concerning his execution, it is generally felt that he was openly unsympathetic with the political regime of that country.

This dispatch would have been followed by a half-dozen other reports from various world trouble-spots. All the smart new words from the current glossary of political science would be used—*terrorist, unprovoked, threatening, nationalistic, the Geneva Accord*. This would be followed by local news, weather, and sports. Then, after a sandwich and a glass of milk, we would turn off our TVs and go to bed. It is sad that we have weaned ourselves from our need of his sacrifice. We have wrapped our passion in apathy. We sleep untroubled before the Cross. No need to confess our sin because we have abandoned the idea of sin. We have "self-esteemed" our way into the court of God, and now we sit at tea with the Almighty and never notice that we are "wretched, pitiful, poor, blind and naked" (Rev. 3:17 NIV).

The Glaucoma of Narcissism

Blinded by the glaucoma of our self-importance, we no longer see the Cross's relevance or significance. There is such

25

an abundance of human suffering in our world that the Cross, were it to happen now, would seem to us far more categorical than unique.

Is the Cross truly the juncture between heaven and hell? During the Exodus, Moses fastened the brazen serpent to a pole and lifted it up to the Israelites who had been bitten by serpents of rebuke (Num. 21:6–9). In the Cross, God stands it up again in our very midst. To merely look is to live. Looking seems so small a price to pay for life. Still, it's the way God does things. He hangs a crude brass snake on a stick and commands us, "Look and live!" It's a good deal—a simple way to end our complex lostness. We ought to instantly obey. But pride is our great deterrent—our refusal to admit we are in need. Fang-marked and envenomed with death, we glance everywhere except at the snake of brass—our only hope. Still God is firm in the matter: Our living lies in our looking.

> WE OUGHT TO INSTANTLY OBEY. BUT PRIDE IS OUR GREAT DETERRENT— OUR REFUSAL TO ADMIT WE ARE IN NEED.

I never will forget that first plain Pentecostal service I attended as a nine-year-old boy. The evangelist—a rural Oklahoma icon of red, weathered skin and fervent emotion— preached on the Cross of Christ. I now know he likely melodramatized the event, but to his credit, I saw for the first time that my transgression was part of the crushing agony that slew my greatest lover. I had been bitten: Even at nine I could see I was dying. But the brazen serpent hung in hopeful, heavy coils that drew the venom from my life and cleansed me in a single look. The Cross did its ageless work. I saw. He came. He conquered. The Cross remains as vivid for me now as it did in that first saving glimpse. My world was as small then as Garfield County, Oklahoma. Yet, believe me when I say that I knew—instantly—that the Cross knew no geography. It was global. It was cosmic. I was overwhelmed by its immortal proportion and by my widening vision of the skully hill where Jesus died for me.

Now I know grace for its true glory. Then I knew enough to understand that Golgotha was not in Garfield County. I also knew Jesus had died in a time far distant from mine. But gathered around me at the altar were all those local saints weeping over his death; I knew I must weep, too, for this was bigger and more sweeping in its importance than anything I had ever known.

The Hound of Calvary

Years later I would learn that the German word *Heilsgeschicte* meant "saving history." I would then understand that history could be recounted in two ways. Its story could be the mere tale of human beings. Or it could be told in terms of God's never-ending pursuit of the human race. And how he does pursue us! Francis Thompson wrote so long ago:

> *I fled Him, down the nights and down the days;*
> *I fled Him, down the arches of the years;*
> *I fled Him, down the labyrinthine ways*
> *Of my own mind; and in the mist of tears*
> *I hid from Him, and under running laughter.*
> *Up vistaed slopes, I sped; and shot, precipitated.*
> *Adown Titanic glooms of chasmed fears.*
> *From those strong Feet that followed, followed after.*[3]

God is both the Hound of Heaven and the Hound of Calvary who pursues each of us through our particular corridor of time. One by one, he tracks us down until, seized by a loving God, we poor humans are made rich by a single look that enables us to live.

In a way, all new believers are children, and most children are naive. Yet Jesus said, "Allow them to come to me, for of such is the kingdom of God" (Matt. 19:14). Why such praise for the naive? Because the Cross finds fertile socket in the tenderness of those who raise it in honor. It is virtually ignored by those who arrogantly feel themselves intellectually mature. Jesus knew that it is the simple heart of a child that thrills in beholding the conquering work of God.

Sing above the battle strife—
Jesus saves! Jesus saves!
By his death and endless life—
Jesus saves! Jesus saves![4]

And so it was that long ago I joined those who sang in a very small clap-sided, one-room church about an event so cosmic in its power that it ransomed all of us.

Just how big is the Cross? One Hebrew word would teach me the size of its glory: *yasha*. This word, I learned a decade later, means "salvation"—it really means "to create room, to make space, as if by knocking down walls."

To look is not just to live, but to thrive in a wall-less world. Here is the glory of the Cross: It bludgeons ghettos, removes fences, and erases boundaries. It calls all littleness to stare at a world large enough to permit any wonder. The Cross saves us by pushing back the walls of prejudice and small thinking. It saves us

THE CROSS FINDS FERTILE SOCKET IN THE TENDERNESS OF THOSE WHO RAISE IT IN HONOR.

by pushing back the stockades of our narrow egos. It flattens our Jerichos until we stand blinking in the brightest sunlight imaginable. The Cross is theological salvation, but it is also sociological and psychological salvation. When I am prone to hate or condemn others, I hear Paul saying, "Who is he that condemneth? It is Christ that died" (Rom. 8:34 KJV). At the Cross my sickly sociology is made well. At the Cross my egotistic psychology is exposed by his light; and it is there that I see the dying Savior and know that I must be crucified with Christ in order to live (Gal. 2:20).

The Cross is the look-and-live event that saves my days as it saves my soul. Because of my own crucified living, I can redeem the time. I can save the very seconds of my service to offer them as a present unto God. Further, I see time as something *I* am running out of, but not God. It is never in short supply for him. God stood the Cross in the center of historical time—time as we see it, use it, and sometimes squander it. But for God, the Cross stands above time, for God lives with no deadlines to hurry him along the corridors of eternity.

Make Yourself Taller—Stand Up Straight

The crucifixion is now over by two thousand years. But in the centuries that preceded it, God sent a vanguard of prophets to announce its arrival. Jeremiah, without mentioning the Cross, clearly outlined its benefits: "Behold, the days come, saith the LORD, that I will make a new covenant with the house of Israel.... This shall be the covenant that I will make with the house of Israel.... I will put my law in their inward parts, and write it in their hearts; and will be their God, and they shall be my people" (Jer. 31:31, 33 KJV). The Cross, as Jeremiah saw it, is God's new covenant. It is Yahweh's new agreement. It is God's "new deal"—God's new deal for me!

What was his "old deal" for me? Well, God has a yardstick graduated from one to ten. Listed by each of the graduations is one of his commandments which he asks me to keep inviolate. The graduations are perfectly calibrated and exact. There is absolutely nothing wrong with his yardstick. The problem is that I am too short. I can't measure up.

But somewhere in that mystical presence that is the mind of God there existed a plan to measure me differently. Oh, he would use the yardstick, to be sure. But he himself would lay before me that yardstick—a cross upon which he, through the miracle of incarnation, had died. Now I can stand on the Cross. By stepping upon this holy wood, I can be elevated enough to measure up to God's expectations.

Paul points out our glorious new stature! "No one," he says, "will be declared righteous in his sight by observing the law.... For all have sinned and fall short of the glory of God, and are justified freely by his grace through...a sacrifice of atonement, through faith in his blood" (Rom. 3:20, 23–25 NIV). To measure up is wonderful! We have been saved not by the Ten Commandments that we could never keep, but by the Cross that keeps *us* and presents us faultless (without sin) and with great joy to our Savior (Jude 24–25).

But what does this really mean—this standing on the Cross that allows us to gain stature? It means that in the greatness of this drama, we learn our true size. We are not to see his Cross as titanic and ourselves as but worms—as some theologians once taught—but we are to see our neediness and his immensity. At the Cross, humility is easy to assume. Why? Because here we need not try to reduce our importance by sighing, "Oh, to be nothing, nothing." Rather, we have only to stand next to the magnificence of Christ, and our own moral shabbiness will be instantly obvious. Humility is never self-depreciation. It is but gaining the true view of ourselves by standing next to his finished majesty. Then, like the centurion, we cry, "Surely this was the Son of God!" (Matt. 27:54), and at the same time we cry, "Surely this is me!" Then like the teenage Isaiah, we cry honestly, "Woe is me, for I am lost! I am a man of unclean lips" (Isa. 6:5).

The Cross in the Subway

Some time ago in New York City, a man was trying to board a subway with his wife. In the rush and hurry of the busy hour, she stepped quickly into one of the coaches of the train. Her husband, pushing and shoving to get in, didn't quite make it. The door of the train closed on his arm. Try as he might, he could not free his arm from the locked door. Then he shuddered as he felt the brakes release and the train lurch. His wife, seeing his condition, began screaming. She could neither free his arm from the door nor get the train stopped.

The poor man tried in vain to anchor himself to something on the station platform. As the train pulled away, he began running, but only at the very first was he able to keep up with the train. In a terrible, horrible instant, the coach in which his arm was caught was flogging him at rapid speeds against the concrete abutments of the subway tube. The train stopped too late. The man died, accidentally caught in the press of people, all going somewhere unimportant. The event got only spotted news coverage.

HUMILITY IS NEVER SELF-DEPRECIATION. IT IS BUT GAINING THE TRUE VIEW OF OURSELVES BY STANDING NEXT TO HIS FINISHED MAJESTY.

To most, it was a tiny tragedy of little significance. The underground trains stopped only long enough to carry the body from the tunnel. Then once again they rattled and banged their way through those infinite miles of sunless tubes. One person among tens of thousands who ride the iron serpents had accidentally been killed by a malfunctioning machine.

I must be careful not to view the Cross in such a way. I must never see Jesus as one little man accidentally trapped in the mechanism of Hebrew custom and Roman politics. Such is not the case. The Cross was programmed exactly as it happened—and all for me. Mysteriously and wonderfully, without ever knowing the program, Herod, Pilate, and the mob followed it. Jesus truly was "the Lamb slain before the foundation of the world" (Rev. 13:8). There was nothing haphazard or accidental in his dying. The Cross was accomplished for my salvation by blueprints that were older than this world.

The Cross over Vanity Fair

The cost of the Cross was immense. Its expense was so great that now the greatest sin we may commit is trying to measure up to God's expectation without its advantage. There is no other way to God. All other roads, however clearly marked, lead only to the "Slough of Despondency" or to "Vanity Fair."

> Jesus, keep me near the cross—
> There a precious fountain,
> Free to all, a healing stream,
> Flows from Calv'ry's mountain.[5]

There is no way to God that does not depend on nails,

thorns, ropes, and wood. There, where the soldiers gambled over garments and the priests mocked a dying carpenter, is the very place where God makes his agreement with us.

Vengeance was there robed in retaliation. Judas may have retaliated because he felt that Jesus liked the other apostles more than him. The Romans retaliated because they hated all Jews. The Pharisees hated Jesus, for he struck out at their hypocrisy. The Sadducees hated him, for he drew people away from their doctrines. The Herodians feared him, for they misunderstood the nature of his kingship.

So their lust for vengeance burned against Jesus. It was their Gordian knot of human pettiness that bound him to his cross: that "get even" desire that Adam passed on to all of us. It was that same desire that had kept Esau lying in wait for his brother Jacob for years. It was the same spirit of vengeance that the young David held in his heart when he slew the giant oppressor of his people. It was the one dream of sightless old Samson, grinding in the prison house, dreaming in darkness of the day when he would avenge Philistia for the last time.

Paul strongly rebuked the Corinthians for coming to that Cross-enriched symbol called communion and hating and quarreling beneath love's finest ensign (1 Cor. 11:17–22). Hate is the great antithesis of the Cross. Love is the only human emotion that may traffic the *Via Dolorosa*.

Bloody Cure for Cynicism

Only once in my life have I been hated by another Christian. It was chilling! Yet much more than hate abused the suffering Christ, as heartless anger and blind hostility were hurled at him from all directions. A few times I have seen Christians caught up in vendettas of ugliness and hatred one for another. They seem so blind to the love of their dying Savior. While salvation is the loss of walls, hate rebuilds those walls with the remnants of old ego.

Grudges and bitterness defile the saving work of Christ. I well remember a woman whose ill will toward a sister led her ultimately to a savage burglary of her hated sister's home. Once inside the home, she destroyed property and defaced family portraits. To what extent will bitterness track hate? Hebrews 12:15 says that it will destroy all his precious dying work.

HOW DID JESUS REACT TO THIS UNITED SPIRIT OF HATE? HE FORGAVE!

But this is the glorious truth: The Cross can deal with malice because it was raised in the very center of human hate. How did Jesus react to this united spirit of hate? He forgave! And then from the Cross he offered God's "new deal" to a thief and a Roman legionary. Hate had scourged love. Hate had ringed love with thorns. Hate had pierced, torn, and mocked love. But love won! It continues to win!

There love hangs, loving the haters, dying for the assassins, caring for the unconcerned, bleeding for the wounded.

The blood of Christ is the witness of God to the triumph of love. The blood of Christ is God's signature on his new agreement with us. The blood means that God means business and the agreement is valid. Once in my journal, near Easter, I wrote:

Can you hear it dripping crimson?
Splashing color into a vivid world?
Dripping warmth over a frigid social system?
Dripping life into the walking corpses
Of the twentieth-century's aching vacuum?
Steadily it falls from the massive wooden beams of the Cross;
Two hundred decades have not arrested its incessant flow;
Tyrants and wars have not plugged the supply;
Steadily it drips in a divine rhythm of redemption.
Stop Niagara if you must!
But you will never stop the drops of eternal love;
They will flow while one heart yet knows how to hate.

A Life-for-Life Agreement

God is in earnest. With all the seriousness of Gethsemane, he offers us this new agreement. But an agreement is never established by just one party. An agreement is the meeting of two minds. The agreement is not completed when God offers us life through the Cross; it is complete only when we accept it.

Golgotha is not a Bavarian passion play where the actors mimic the final chapters of the Book of Matthew and charge us so much per seat. It is God, caught up in the violence of life and death, who extends to us the benefits of Christ's sufferings.

Essentially, this new covenant is God's saying, "I want your life for the life of my Son." It is a life-for-life agreement; we must be willing to give God all we have, since God gave us all that *he* had. We cannot consider how much it will cost to participate in the agreement, for he did not count the cost. We are to obey him, even as the Son obeyed his Father.

> GOD WILL CUT NO DEALS WITH US FOR HALF A LIFE. HE WILL NOT BARGAIN ON PROPORTIONATE DEDICATION.

Here at the Cross, all the issues are drawn in superlatives. God will cut no deals with us for half a life. He will not bargain on proportionate dedication. With him it is either all or nothing. If we are not prepared to offer him everything, we must not waste our time offering him anything. To discover the joy of God's new agreement, we must come to him with this kind of prayer:

Dear Lord of the New Agreement,

They are yours—these hands of mine that have dipped into the mire of sin, these feet of mine that have too long walked in their own way.

Here, Lord! Accept these lips that have dealt so often in lies and curses.

Is this heart of mine so hardened by spiritual sclerosis that it cannot beat in soft compassion?

I bring you so little. I'm such an imperfect piece of clay, but the whole mold is yours, God!

Let everyone say there isn't much, but let no one say it isn't all.

Thou didst not come down
from the cross when they
shouted to thee, mocking
and reviling thee,
"Come down from the cross
and we will believe that
Thou art He."
Thou didst not come down,
for again Thou wouldst not
enslave men by a miracle,
and didst crave faith freely
given, not based on miracle.

Fyodor Dostoevsky
THE GRAND INQUISITOR

CHAPTER THREE

The Timbers of Grief

THE CROSS ANSWERS OUR GRIEVING

Near the cross of Jesus stood his mother, his mother's sister, Mary the wife of Clopas, and Mary Magdalene. When Jesus saw his mother there, and the disciple whom he loved standing nearby, he said to his mother, "Dear woman, here is your son," and to the disciple, "Here is your mother." From that time on, this disciple took her into his home. (John 19:25–27 NIV)

Once upon a tree, there was a man. Over the tree there hung a sign announcing in the bold letters of three languages the verdict that had ordered his suffering. Beneath the tree stood the grieving mother of the heretic. She was a woman whose face was rimmed by little wisps of silver hair that protruded defiantly from under her mantle; occasionally she trembled with uncontrollable spasms of despair. Before the tree a young fisherman gazed in blurred glances at his dying friend; his broad arm cradled the head of the convict's mother. But he was unable to console her. The man on the cross was her son. Yet his strong, young arm rippled with the kind of strength that might sustain a mother blinded by the sight of her son on the gallows.

41

I am intrigued and ashamed by the Cross. Its offense enthralls me. I bless it while I cry for its injustice. I need his blood yet know it cost so much more than I am worth—still he thought I was worth it.

When Michelangelo carved his *Pietà*, he carved Mary two-thirds larger than she should have been. Why? Because he wished us to envision her as a giantesque madonna, holding her executed son with the largesse of a dowager queen ripped of soul by contemplating the cruelty of Earth. But Michelangelo was wrong about this. Grief does not enlarge us; it shrinks our souls.

WHAT IS THERE IN THIS SAD PORTRAIT THAT IS THE BEGINNING OF A GREAT WORLD FAITH?

The real Mary was diminished by her agony. The real Mary *grieved*. She did not feel large that day, but very small—a soul of no consequence lost in a human machine. The crucifixion of her son did not empower her; it debilitated her. Perhaps as she wept that Good Friday she remembered Simeon's words of prophecy, spoken to her years ago when she took the infant Jesus into the temple: "And a sword will pierce your own soul too" (Luke 2:35b NIV). The word for *sword* Simeon used is the Greek word *romphaia*, a huge Persian sword that literally skewers its victims in pain.

Grief is always a *romphaia* in our lives. I remember a neighbor woman whose son had been a chum of mine. The boy shocked us all by being involved in a terrible crime for which he was sentenced to prison. On the day of his sentencing, I saw and understood Simeon's *romphaia*. I saw the sword of grief run this poor woman through as they took her son away.

The Claims of the Crucified Man

Here at Calvary I behold a pitiable trio: a dying carpenter, his sorrowing mother, and his idealistic young friend. What is there in this sad portrait that is the beginning of a great world faith? After all, Mary was not the first mother to lose a son, nor would she be the last. The answer to the question may well be connected to the sign fastened to the top of the cross. This sign labeled with ancient characters was a proclamation that distinguished the death of Jesus from all other cases of bereavement. "Jesus of Nazareth, King of the Jews" read the sign. The inscription was one of the claims the crucified man had made. This claim, along with others, had so angered the professional religionists that in the spirit of unorganized rioting, they had picked up thorns, a whip, a robe of mockery, and other ingredients of cross-making.

> *In this of Christ I glory,*
> *Standing dumb before his story.*
> *I see the nails and wonder at the grace.*
> *Dare I lift my eyes to look on such a face?*[1]

The inscription over the cross transforms his dying into a great stop sign on the pointless roadway of my life. It is that one great visible symbol that dominates our churches, challenging us with the dailyness of Luke 9:23. I daily face a question only arrogance could answer: Am I bearing my cross, dying daily that he might live and proclaim himself sovereign over every involvement of my life?

What brought about the crucifixion and the grief felt by Jesus' friend and mother? We know that Jesus had gotten himself into trouble with the religious leaders because of what he claimed. What were those claims? What do his claims mean for me?

To begin with, we need to remember that Jesus claimed to have no earthly father. "The Jews then murmured at him, because he said, I am the bread which came down from heaven. And they said, Is not this Jesus, the son of Joseph, whose father and mother we know? how is it then that he saith, I came down from heaven?" (John 6:41–42 KJV). Then, too, he claimed to be the Messiah prophesied of old. He claimed that he was the King of Kings and would rise again on the third day after his death. Finally, there was the claim that resulted in his execution: He called himself the Son of God—even at his trial! (Luke 22:70).

The Cross was supposed to silence all his claims. Instead, it substantiated them. So rather than railing at the Cross with scorn, I must salute it. I dare not look at it through eyes of hate; I must exalt it as ultimate love. I never cry that the Cross is wretched, but that *I* am. Since that fateful day, I have joined a stream of souls, two thousand years long, each apologizing to the Cross for the sinful and unbelieving part of my own nature that produced it. And so that rough sign, too hastily lettered with ancient glyphs, has proven true—Jesus is King!

God Never Says Much on Good Fridays

At the Cross, I must deal with the majesty of his claims. Was he the Son of God or not? Was he the Messiah, or was he mistaken? Was he the Savior, or was he schizophrenic? One thing is clear: Jesus is either the most important person in all of history or a psychotic serving his immense delusions of grandeur. There is no halfway point between these extremes. On the issue of Christ's identity, we cannot have it both ways: maybe saint, maybe psychotic. His claims leave us with no compromised conviction. No middle ground. We are either most wise for believing his claims or fools for revering his delusions. Where are the credentials that support his outlandish claims? The Cross alone is the affirmation for all he claimed.

Jesus claimed to be God's Son. His executioners said that the very fact that he did not come down from the cross was evidence that he was not the Son of God—son of Joseph perhaps, or son of Mary, but not the Son of God (Matt. 27:43). We must admit that God seems strangely silent as Jesus dies. It appears as though Jesus died alone—all alone. And the loneliness of his dying only deepens our

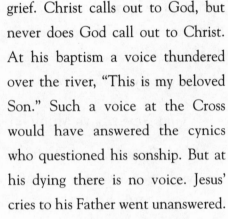

IF YOU DO NOT
ANSWER YOUR
OWN SON, HOW
CAN I BELIEVE
YOU WILL
ANSWER ME?

grief. Christ calls out to God, but never does God call out to Christ. At his baptism a voice thundered over the river, "This is my beloved Son." Such a voice at the Cross would have answered the cynics who questioned his sonship. But at his dying there is no voice. Jesus' cries to his Father went unanswered. This must have seemed to some the plaintive cry of a new orphan not yet able to absorb the fact that his parents are dead.

Crosses are places where God always seems silent, so we cry, "Forsaken...forsaken...forsaken! Why, God, why?" But while we agonize over "why?" we hear only the sound of the wind and our own labored, suffocating breath! Like Jesus, we have our own private calvaries. In watching Christ die, we realize that life is not all that easy for us either. The silence of God in our own separate crucifixions results in our giving God a lot of bad press. We're dying while the ropes chafe and the nails tear; as we cry, he retreats.

One of my friends died of cancer. As the spreading adder inside her body twisted and constricted, she lifted her eyes to her only hope of life—God. I prayed for her and cried; I wept and entreated. But God was silent.

The mind of the skeptic indicts the silence of God even from the midst of the predicament. The words mock our Father even as they probe the quiet: "Is there no answer for your Son, God? Is it because he is not your Son? For three years now, Jesus has everywhere claimed you as his Father. Listen to his plaintive cry, 'My God, my God, why hast thou forsaken me?' (Matt. 27:46 KJV). Will you not answer him, God? Then surely you are not his true Father. His true Father would not forsake him. Further God, if you do not answer your own Son, how can I believe you will answer me?" I dare not be too brazen with God, for I know his Cross interprets all silence.

As Jesus' cry of loneliness faded into stillness, there was nothing but the whisper of afternoon breeze and the scream of the carrion eagles, circling in the sickly sky above the tree. But Jesus' tormentors were wrong in their conclusions. There is always a time when the silence ends. There is always a time when God answers evil!

God in the Gloom of the Tomb

In the case of the Cross, God breaks the silence not with words but with midnight. He blotted out his sun so that "there was a darkness over all the earth until the ninth hour" (Luke 23:44 KJV). But God's darkness was not brutal —it was rather a drape of friendly shadows that hid the naked shame of his beloved. The cruel crucifiers who came in God's light to gloat victoriously over the martyrdom of Jesus would not have his light to see them home. His darkness matched the blindness of human hearts. In this darkness, God opened graves and living dead men shuffled through the afternoon gloom. Those who were bringing death to his Son met death in the streets, for men and half-men, reeking with mildew and decay, walked the market-place and byways. Such was God's answer to the executioners of his Son: silence broken by the shuffling of twilight corpses.

But God had one more answer left for the religious leaders who felt they had done God service by nailing his Son to a cross. These blind guides called themselves men of God but they did not understand that when they stripped and crucified Jesus, they stole God's dignity too. So God replied to their desecration. Inside the fabulous temple, erected at great expense for his worship, God devoured their pride.

The lavish draperies that hung before the Holy of Holies were indescribably beautiful, rich with color and ornate bro-cade. This huge valance prefaced the inner sanctum of the temple. The curtain was designed to enshrine the very seat of God's presence on earth—the Ark of the Covenant.

These immense, heavy hangings were there to veil the holiness of God from unholy men. But as surely as if it had been old linen, God ripped the tapestries of the temple and threw them aside. He would not have men covering and honoring his holiness within the temple while they mocked and exposed it on a hilltop outside the city.

God's Sorrow

Perhaps you find yourself asking, "Why the darkness? Why set the living dead to walking in the city? Why was the temple veil shredded?" There are probably two reasons. First of all, God was crying. This is how God cries when his Son dies unloved and alone.

The grieving God is a God whose Spirit I often invoke in the lives of those I care for. I well remember a young boy in our church who was playing in the street. He was impaled on the stiletto hood ornament of a speeding car. His death was instant. His parents were first stunned and later filled with grief, and finally, they were hostile toward God.

But because of the grief of God, I could say to them, "Do not be angry at heaven! God also lost a boy. He understands. Don't be mad at him; rather reach out to him." Hebrews 12:1–3 talks of how men and women of faith look toward Jesus: the pioneer, the *archegos*, the "first-goer." When we must enter the shadow of hurt, we are relieved to see ahead of our plodding pain the footfalls of Jesus, the *archegos* who pioneered the valley of grief. Gethsemane's terror caused Jesus to "sweat" great drops of blood. It was not fear but grief, I think, that brought his agony.

In Ephesians 4:30, the apostle Paul tells me not to grieve the Holy Spirit, with whom I am sealed to the day of redemption. Not only did Good Friday grieve the heart of the Father; God's grief continues in the current moments of my infidelity. *Grieve* is a love word. When I willfully disobey God, it is not as though I anger him; it is rather that I hurt him.

When my mother died, I felt immediately the anguish of heart that God must feel in his grief at the Cross. But I could turn to God and hear him say "Come unto me, all ye that labour and are heavy laden" (Matt. 11:28 KJV) or "Casting all your care upon him; for he careth for you" (1 Pet. 5:7 KJV) or "We do not have a God who is unable to be touched with feelings of our infirmities" (Heb. 4:15). This *archegos* God reminded me that he had been to the mourner's pyre long before me. During those dark days, the words of a wonderful hymn came to my consciousness:

> Come, ye disconsolate, where'er ye languish;
> Come to the mercy seat, fervently kneel;
> Here bring your wounded hearts, here tell your anguish;
> Earth has no sorrow that heav'n cannot heal.[2]

Why is it that heaven can heal earth's heartaches? Because God did not sidestep earth's agony. He permitted himself no luxuries or easy times. He was the first-goer who allowed himself to know grief centuries ahead of us. As God submitted his Almighty Being to grief, so we are instructed to adore and praise the God who suffers.

You may feel that God took it all a bit hard. After all, he knew that Jesus' suffering was only temporary. He knew that Easter would gobble up Good Friday and that the triumph would be eternal. Did God have to rip the temple veil and rail against the crucifiers with thunder and earthquake?

GOD SUBMITTED HIS ALMIGHTY BEING TO GRIEF.

Perhaps it was only for a day or so, but the physiology of pain and death was all very real. Jesus was fully man, and his fully human nervous system was set ablaze with torture. God is in this sense like any good father. Good fathers weep when their sons suffer.

No wonder the Book of Revelation focuses on that day when "God shall wipe away all tears from their eyes, neither shall there be any more crying" (Rev. 21:4). We grieve because something valuable has been taken away and is lost.

Sometimes in shopping malls a child wriggles free and is lost. Panic and grief seize the parent, and the parent runs. But in which direction? Who would know where that lost child is? Can you not see why the word *lost* is a word that grieves the heart of God? When Jesus says "For the Son of Man came to seek and to save what was lost" (Luke 19:10 NIV), we see the dilemma of a parent who is frantic over a missing child. God, too, grieves human lostness, "not willing that any should perish" (2 Peter 3:9 KJV).

Dr. Thomas Dooley, in his book *The Night They Burned the Mountain*, tells a correlating story that well illustrates the grief of God when we endure hopelessness or pain. One of the Laotians had given him a tiny Himalayan moonbear. It was a cuddly ball of brown fur, full of interesting antics, and Dr. Dooley set to building a cage for the animal. An old Chinese man happened upon him as he worked on the cage and stared at him in disbelief. The old man began to sob, and when Dr. Dooley sought to discover the reason for his tears, the man told him that the cage was reminiscent of the greatest tragedy he had ever experienced. The old Chinese and his son had once worked together on a commune in Red China. He reminded the good doctor that laborers on the communes at harvesttime were not to have one grain of rice for themselves, for it was all the property of the Republic. The son of this old man had disobeyed the harvest mandate. Since his mother was sick with beriberi and malnutrition, the son had concealed a few handfuls of rice in his clothing to take to his starving mother. He was, of course, discovered, and the authorities made a public whipping boy out of him. They imprisoned him in a cage, not unlike the one that Dr. Dooley had made for his pet bear, and had put the caged youth in the center of the city.

The cage was so small that the boy could not move or even sit up straight. The old man's testimony went like this: "His mother and I were forced to watch, she from one side of the square and I from the other. But the guards would not allow us to go near him. Day after day, as we looked on, my boy died slowly, under the broiling sun with nothing to eat or drink, covered with filth, flies and ants. It was good when the guards pronounced him dead."[3] The man had since escaped from China, but the very sight of a cage aroused his torturous memory once more.

Our basic emotions are the way we demonstrate that we are people—real live human beings. If we appear callous in the face of agony's great grief, others will say that we are inhuman. The very word *compassion* means "to suffer with." This phrase is used of Jesus many times in the Gospels. Jesus was always moved with compassion. He would not let people grieve alone. Nor will God permit you a single tear he does not long to wipe away. On the cross, when he says to John, "Son, behold your mother. Mother, behold your son," he is saying to both of them, "Mary and John, never allow the other to suffer alone."

We dehumanize people when we are too busy to be counselors to their hurt. Paul reminds me that I must not "grieve as those who have no hope" (1 Thess. 4:13). At the base of this command lies the remembrance that I, too, am called to bear up my world by ministering to those who grieve. God is the Almighty Consoler in the thunder and quake of his Calvary grief.

If our compassion defines the heart of God in Christ, then what does our indifference do? "Please care!" is the cry of our alienated society. "Please care!" is the ink on every suicide note. Fifty-eight thousand Americans died in the Vietnam conflict; then nine thousand Vietnam veterans have committed suicide since the war ended. What lived in the hearts of those who died when the battle was over? Why was life so distasteful that they later killed themselves? Were they slain ahead of time by seeing too much death around them and too much indifference at home?

I want to feel the Savior as he dies; I want my spirit to resonate with his as the cross juts up amidst the deserting apostles and the sparse crowd on the hilltop. I once rode on an airplane with a young man whose whole frame was shaking with sobs. I audaciously put my arm around him. It took courage, for he was a complete stranger. He told me between sobs that he was twenty years old and that every other member of his family had just been killed in an automobile accident. Why was I so bold as to reach out to his crying? At the Cross, God teaches me that grief should not go unattended.

God's Answer

There is, of course, a second reason for the unnatural display of darkness and fury that was God's response to the

Cross. It was not merely God's sorrow. It was his power! The display was God's answer to the skeptics. Those who stood by reasoned with natural logic: "If he is God's Son, why doesn't God do something?" So, God did something! And by those very things he did, he seemed to be saying, "I am his Father; he is my Son. All he said was true."

God shook his planet with an earthquake, and the rocks were split (Matt. 27:51). He shook it lightly, to be sure, for his Son had nails in his hands. God drew a veil of heavy thunderheads across the afternoon sun and spoke with the suddenness of crashing thunder. We still stand dumb before his power.

> AT THE CROSS,
> GOD TEACHES ME
> THAT GRIEF
> SHOULD NOT GO
> UNATTENDED.

God succeeded in validating Jesus' claim to be the Son of God. Standing near the cross was a soldier, whose daring whisper of truth was heard above the clamor of unbelieving slander. He was impressed with Jesus' meekness. He marveled at his calm on the timbers of death. Then, when all nature seemed to invert itself and the heavens shook above the cross and the earth quaked beneath it, the soldier breathed the validity of Jesus' claim, "Truly this *was* the Son of God" (Matt. 27:54 KJV).

Here it was that life began for the centurion. When the behavior of nature was disorderly and all creation seemed topsy-turvy, a soldier made the claim for Jesus that Jesus so often had made for himself. So life began for this nameless centurion who voiced earth's conviction—Jesus is the Son of God, and God is the Mighty One who establishes creation's order—or overthrows it if he wishes.

The Logic of Disbelief

If you do not accept what the centurion embraced as truth, it may be that your circumstances are too different. Perhaps you confront the Cross too logically in the midst of easy living. You are free to examine Golgotha in the comfort of overstuffed furniture or while listening to the sweetness of organ music played at the church's annual Easter service. In these conditions you are undecided about it all. This type of comfortable analysis may never lead you to say, "Surely, this was the Son of God!"

But if you were to accost it exactly as the centurion did, with the unsteady earth reeling beneath your feet and the gray sky thundering judgment, you would more likely come to belief. In a split instant, this soldier's heart reached out to provide ballast for his mind. His trembling lips issued the affirmation that the man on the cross was God's Son. If to no one else, at least to him, Christ was very God. The Cross itself had made that clear. If it was clear to the centurion, then it must be to us. There at "the place of the skull," God stood by the assertion that Jesus so often made—he was the Son of God.

A second reason for not instantly calling Jesus the Son of God may be that you have not yet been debilitated by need or pain. We cannot know what the centurion's needs were. Had he experienced grief or loss? Who can say? But grief or loss makes us open to calling Jesus the Son of God.

Christ made other claims that the Cross certified as truth. Christ came among us calling God "Father" and teaching us that God loved us as a parent loves, only infinitely deeper. He said early in his ministry to Nicodemus, the Hebrew statesman, "For God so loved the world, that he gave his only begotten Son, that whosoever believeth in him should not perish, but have everlasting life" (John 3:16 KJV). Did God mean it? Did he really love humanity that much? The Cross says he did.

God's Bloody Friday Options

Calvary is the dilemma of divine love. God loved us, and he loved his Son. Who can measure the anguish that tore its jagged way through celestial love when God's beloved Son was on the tree. As Creator, he dared to leave him there. It has been said that when the cross was jolted in its socket, ten thousand angels drew swords against an unfeeling planet. But God spared his precious world their wrath. Jesus claimed God's love for us, and God demonstrated it on Good Friday.

IN THE SECLUSION OF AN OLIVE GROVE, THE FATHER AND HIS SON HAD AGREED ON THE FINAL ISSUES OF DELIVERANCE FOR THIS PLANET EARTH.

Gethsemane was really the testing place for God's "Son-love" and God's "world-love." In the seclusion of an olive grove on Thursday, the Father and his Son had agreed on the final issues of deliverance for this planet Earth. Although both sought to avoid the extremities of the test, there was not a minor discord anywhere in the harmony of their wills. They were united in the task of redeeming a wayward world. God assured the Son that if at any time he wished to escape the agony, one cry to the Father would have instantly delivered him and cursed the world with eternal hopelessness and death. But the dutiful, compassionate Son, knowing his Father's love for us, had set his face like a flint to serve God's world-love, and he would not swerve from the dream.

Do you realize what this means? It means that God could have saved either us *or* his Son. Yet he and his Son together, at the expense of the Son, chose to save us. How much he must love us! It was not a project in which the Father was uninvolved. God also felt the stigma of mockery. He, too, stumbled along the Way of Sorrows. The ghastly crown sliced at his kingship too. He and his Son were cosufferers. In the fondest hope that we might truly become his children, God let his own Child die. There is no cold piece of philosophy that can do away with this. The Cross is the tangible, historical evidence that God loves us. It does not say *why* God loves us, but it does answer "How much?" Paul said the same thing when he wrote "For at the very time when we were still powerless, then Christ died for the wicked. Even for a just man one of us would hardly die, though perhaps for a good man one might actually brave death; but Christ died for us while we were yet sinners, and that is God's own proof of his love towards us" (Rom 5:6–8 NEB).

Once upon a tree, God proved his world-love. It was the most powerful way he could say, "I love you."

The Way of the Cross

There is yet one other claim that the crucifixion affirms—the importance of our grieving. Jesus once said, "I am the way, the truth, and the life: no man cometh unto the Father, but by me" (John 14:6 KJV). What a fantastic claim! Think of the enormity of it! He did not say, "I am *a* way to God," but "I am *the* way." There is no way to God that bypasses the Son, claimed Christ. This exclusivist doctrine of Christianity has led many to say that not only was Jesus deluded about himself, but that he was a conceited bigot (one of the worst names one can be called in this go-along-with-it generation). This exclusive teaching cut like a rawhide lash across the unfeeling flesh of Pharisaism. It still offends all those who seek some lesser pathway to God.

There are a thousand prophets and as many cults that outline some course of "meaningfulness" that does not involve the grief of dying. Some intellectuals, unable to fold the majestic claims and deeds of Jesus into their alkaline gray matter, turn to pagan mysticism or Oriental asceticism. Meanwhile, practical-minded moralists measure themselves by the vague calibrations on their Golden Ruler, which they have broken and mended half-a-hundred times. Such are our pitiful attempts to arrive at life's meaning on our own. Some ultimately slash their wrists. Others become shells whose inner emptiness is filled with the fading echoes of all that might have been.

> OUR LORD ENDURED THE UGLINESS OF IT ALL, NOT SO I MIGHT HAVE AN ALTERNATE ROUTE OF REDEMPTION, BUT BECAUSE THERE WAS NO OTHER WAY.

Probably the most popular alternative to "the way of the Cross" is the sincerity cult. To the devotees of this cult, doctrine is unimportant. All that matters is sincerity and "good intentions." Even the aborigine with his neck ringed in tiger teeth, if faithful to his amulet, will reach God as surely as the apostle Paul. To many, sincerity and salvation are synonyms. Ignoring the consideration that people can be sincerely wrong, sincerity says, "I may, in truth, be wrong, but Infinite Love will consider my devotion." Such self-styled religion is to be pitied. No wonder some wag has said, "Be sincere, even if you don't mean it!"

Jesus is the only way to God. May Gautama, Confucius, and Mohammed take note: The way to God must pass through Christ and his Cross. Thomas à Kempis made this same claim for Jesus:

> Follow Me: I am the way, the truth, and the life.
>> Without the way there is no going;
>> Without the truth there is no knowing;
>> Without the life there is no living.[4]

But it is the Cross itself that affirms this truth most clearly. The only reason the crucifixion came to be was that there were no alternatives.

I must live free of "sincerity" delusions. If there had been any other way for me to be saved, there would never have been a Calvary. Our Lord endured the ugliness of it all, not so I might have an alternate route of redemption, but because there was no other way. Had there been some less expensive way, the Son would never have gone back to the

Father with scarred hands. Nor would he ever have suffered a naked death before his mother. If there had been any other approach possible, the Lord would have shouted the command to angelic legions, waiting at rapt attention for the call to deliver him.

Christ on His Odyssey of Life

A fable is told of Jesus and Gabriel the archangel: It concerns the Son as he leaves the immaculate state of God's presence to hurl himself into history. Gabriel, at the last of the seven gates, arrests Christ and asks him where he is going. "To Bethlehem of Judah," answers Jesus. Gabriel seems annoyed that anyone would voluntarily leave the Crystal City for any reason, so he asks, "Why?" Jesus replies that the Father loves the world and is sending him to redeem it.

Unable to turn him from his mission, Gabriel watches from the outer portal of the estate, while Jesus folds himself into flesh and is laid by a happy young mother in a manger, among the bleating of sheep and lowing of cattle. Gabriel soon loses sight of it all, but he waits patiently while the months become decades. Eagerly he scans the approaches to the Father's house, joyfully anticipating the sight of Jesus. Then, finally, after thirty-three years of faithful vigilance, Gabriel meets Jesus returning through the celestial pillars. He is horrified as he greets Christ: "Lord, what happened to you down there? Whence came these scars? What fiend would so mistreat the Father's Son? And the world you went to save? Did you save it, Lord?"

Then Jesus speaks, "No, Gabriel, I did not save humanity. I saved only a few, and I saved them by these scars."

"But, Lord," protests the archangel, "what about the rest of humanity? Will they never be redeemed?"

"Gabriel, I left the saving message with a small group of witnesses who have beheld my scars; if the rest of the world is to be saved, it must be saved by these same wounds—there is no other way!"

So, one by one, the Cross cements the certainty of each of the things Christ claimed. The sun went dark to prove he was God's Son, as

WOODEN BEAMS AND HUMAN ANGUISH DEMONSTRATED THE DEPTHS OF GOD'S LOVE FOR HIS WORLD.

he had taught. Wooden beams and human anguish demonstrated the depths of God's love for his world. And, of course, all of it was to say that there is only one way to God. The Cross saves even as it answers our grief.

There is one claim the Cross would yet make—ourselves! He wants the total us, mind you! The sum of all of our possessions, energies, and talents. From the very midst of our tears, we must confess that Christ is God's Son. He has the right to possess our lives.

Man's mind cannot grasp

the causes of events

in their completeness,

but the desire to find

those causes is implanted

in man's soul.

Leo Tolstoy

WAR AND PEACE

CHAPTER FOUR

The Community of the Cross

GOD'S KINGDOM AND COMMUNITY

But when they came to Jesus and found that he was already dead, they did not break his legs. Instead, one of the soldiers pierced Jesus' side with a spear, bringing a sudden flow of blood and water. The man who saw it has given testimony, and his testimony is true. He knows that he tells the truth, and he testifies so that you also may believe. These things happened so that the scripture would be fulfilled: "Not one of his bones will be broken." (John 19:33–36 NIV)

I am a believer. I am therefore a part of the community of the Cross. Here, in this community, we—the previously desperate and the previously lost—come together and rehearse the glory of our kingdom community. I love the hymns, the sermons—even the bad ones—because I remember that I once was lost but now belong to the society of the reclaimed. I am a part of the people of need who have now become the people of grace. In our community the once-hopeless meet, confess their identity, speak of their need, and promise each other support. No wonder D. T. Niles defined the kingdom community as one beggar telling another where to get bread.

How fortunate I am to belong to a group that cares for me and, at the same time, demands care from me. So many men and women, these days, arrive home at night and are swallowed up in loneliness by electric garage doors. They live utterly alone with few friends and little support. But I, by comparison, live a charmed life. My cries ring out above a community of people whom I need and who need me, and as the popular singers testify, "People who need people are the luckiest people in the world."

The community of the Cross is a fellowship of poverty. Years ago Louis Evely called the true church the "fraternity of the poor." He based his view of the church on Jesus' Beatitude: "Blessed are the poor in spirit" (Matt. 5:3 NIV). Only the most spiritually destitute are aware of their needs. Only the poor let those needs draw them together in true community. I, too, came to call him "Lord" because I knew I was destitute. My hopeless poverty had produced in me a great need. My emptiness begged his abundance, and I was gloriously enfranchised.

The Company of the Crucified

We who need him enter his community of love. There we find our finest friends in the hour of our desperation, for when we hurt we find there is a fellowship in suffering (Phil. 3:10). It is no accident that hospitals make inmates of cancer patients, housing them in the same ward. Those who suffer the same kind of pain find the closest kind of identity. It is odd that while the Bible takes no pains to name the two bandits who died with Christ, tradition strongly names one of them as Dismus. Why do we need his name? Or why have we invented it? Because men should not suffer death together without knowing each other's names.

The Cross builds a vibrant community in our midst. Look at the countless ways we refer to our cross-bearing community: "If you don't bear the cross, then you can't wear the crown." "We are crucified with Christ." Even words like *cruciform* and *excruciating* (out of the cross) and *crucible* come from the Latin word for *cross*. As a symbol, the cross dominates our culture.

But as a community member, I am fascinated by the primary models of John and Mary, the believing centurion, and the seeking thief. Along with Nicodemus who begged his body, they are the only friends the Bible mentions as being with Christ at the moment of his death. Of these five, it is only John who might have endangered his life by being present. When Jesus calls his disciples, he calls them not to glory but to a legion of contempt. "Blessed are you when men shall persecute you," he said (Matt. 5:10). But he also said, "If you don't take up the cross, you cannot follow me" (Luke 9:23). If we link these two scriptures together, it is easy to read him as saying "Blessed is he who sits in the company of the crucified ones."

What is the purpose of this Cross-forged company? Does the Cross call us to be only a support team helping other Christians through life? Hardly. The community of the Cross is° called to press the great saving dream of God upon

THE COMMUNITY OF THE CROSS IS CALLED TO PRESS THE GREAT SAVING DREAM OF GOD UPON THE UNREDEEMED WORLD.

the unredeemed world. It is not the will of the Father that any should perish (2 Pet. 3:9). We know that Christ wants to draw all men to his Father that they might be saved (John 6:37). His last instructions to the community were Go into all the world and preach the gospel to every creature (Matt. 28:19–20). The community of the Cross exists to serve its Master in the task of

reclaiming all that Adam lost in the Fall. We are there to bind up the broken and preach deliverance to the captives (Luke 4:18–19), which Jesus said was the reason he came to earth. His community exists to continue his work.

Frontline Fellowship

Each time I go to a church party and hear someone brag about how "good" the church fellowship is, I cringe. Fellowship is not a party. *Koinonia* as fellowship in the biblical sense is a word first used in Luke 5:10 to describe the fishermen apostles as business partners. Our *koinonia* means we are a community business: partners in the glorious calling of reaching out to reclaim God's world.

A. W. Tozer used to speak of both frontline and rearguard *koinonia* fellowship. Rearguard fellowship is Christian fellowship that majors on sociability. Frankly, we all like the rear guard best, for at the rear of the army we are in little danger. Even the battle sounds are faint and far away. The generals and joint chiefs, our favorite friends, are all at the back of the army. Here with the most elite we feel best about ourselves. Here we may have tea and biscuits, secure in the knowledge that we are in no real danger. Here we are the safe armchair soldiers who know friendship and laughter. But this warm way of life is always more hollow than the fellowship at the front lines.

There the roar of shell and the stabbing of hateful bayonets make life so precarious that those soldiers must defend each other at every parry, lest through their unguarded negligence a brother is killed. Those on the front line never enjoy rearguard safety. Nor is their laughter frequent. They live in the trenches, depending upon each other's vigilance to survive. This is what Elton Trueblood once called "the company of the committed." These frontline soldiers I refer to as the community of the Cross.

Our community knows no self-sufficient members. We not only owe our peace of mind to the community, we owe it our entire existence. Self-sufficiency and cross-bearing do not travel together in our "great fraternity of the poor." When Jesus said, "Blessed are the poor in spirit" (Matt. 5:3 NIV), he was blessing those of us who are too emotionally needy to be self-sufficient.

So often I have knelt with my prayer group when my heart was breaking. In my thorn-in-the-flesh condition, I find that God's strength is made perfect in my weakness (2 Cor. 12:7–10), as my community of friends prays for me and lifts me through the support of their spirit. Then I discover why James says, "Confess your faults one to another and pray for one another that you may be healed" (James 5:16). I am part of the community of the Cross. I rejoice in my need, for my need binds me to it.

Can this be why Dismus the thief begs, "Jesus, remember me when you come into your kingdom"? (Luke 23:42 NIV). Alone and dying, his aching shame begs anyone to notice him and reach out to him. Those of us who share the crucified life, the dying life, are often broken souls, and our brokenness is our glory. Our separate crosses draw us toward each other as a company of needy souls, and we cry, "I am crucified with Christ: No other way of life can matter."

Faith: An Application for Pain and Shame

So often I must examine those specific elements of the community that draw me to it. First, there is *pain*. Not much needs to be said specifically about pain at this point, because it will be the theme of chapter 9. But I must at least acknowledge that when I hurt, I reach out. Further, one of the strongest of all bonds of identity exists among those who have walked the same vale of suffering, who have endured an equal immensity of pain.

I recently led a seminar in which two wheelchair-paraplegics rolled into the classroom. They were having a wonderful time—never have I seen two souls who more understood and enjoyed each other's presence. But underneath the richness of their camaraderie, I saw the cross that each of them had encountered and were each day transcending. Pain makes brothers of crucified souls.

Another very potent element of the Cross-community is *shame*. Nakedness spawns an elegance of fellowship unattainable elsewhere. I have often watched the documentaries of Auschwitz and wept for those Jews who by the thousands had their clothing stripped away. Then in their common nakedness, they struggled to find a shred of human dignity. Solzhenitsyn says there is no more fearful experience than to have all your clothing stripped away and then be forced into an interrogation. It is not possible to answer as fully human when the trappings of our dignity are removed. Then we are too small to answer. Then we are less than persons in our own eyes.

It is Jesus who, naked on his cross, provides for me the only response to maintaining my self-esteem in the glaring light of open shame. Some crosses are of our own making—but never mind. Even the crosses we deserve meet the forgiveness of both our Lord and our community. In our community no one points the finger at our stupidity. No one! Seeing our shame raises a chill that makes our friends throw a coverlet around our nakedness. After all, everyone has lapses of stupidity. Our community understands this. All have been forgiven, and all will be forgiving as each of us takes upon ourselves the crucified life.

> SHAME IS THE GREAT UNANSWERABLE REDUCTION. BUT HOW IT PURGES OUR FOOLISH PRIDE!

Shame is the great unanswerable reduction. But how it purges our foolish pride! Suddenly our flesh is bare. Suddenly our need to appear in charge is less than our need to be understood. We have been caught! We are then pronounced "guilty" or "reviled" or "despised," and we cannot answer. But on the back side of our shame, our humanity takes charge of our former arrogance.

I once knew a woman who was unpleasantly "superior" to all those around her. She was avoided—and often hurt—because most people could not tolerate her arrogance. Then she was convicted of a crime and arraigned in court and became the butt of public scandal. Suddenly she was in need, and she did not merely reach for acceptance, she pleaded for it. Of course, she received acceptance, for her need was the object of our concern. She saw how her self-sufficiency was a hollow sham and gladly became part of the community of the Cross.

Paul cried out that Christ's shame is our glory. Yes, he died naked on the cross, but we should glory in his shame. It is in his naked dying that I love the crucified God the most. For in his almighty love, he identified with us at the deepest level of degradation. Isaiah prophesied that he would be "despised and rejected of men" (Isa. 53:3 KJV), and yet he became the glorious center of our community. There is no level of earthly embarrassment we could endure that our Immanuel God has not already suffered. I come again to Christ the *archegos*—our pioneer and first-goer. He went first into the vale of shame; wherever we must go, he has already been—Christ, the first-goer.

Through no fault of his own, one of my friends was forced into police court and publicly named in the newspaper. He felt so ashamed for embarrassing the church. Then one woman in our community told him about a similar period in her life. Her family was smeared by the press and every morning had their pictures in the paper. "Your shame will pass," she said, "and when it does your brothers and sisters will be right here. That's what it means to be a Christian."

Why should the forgiven not be forgiving? Why should

those with older scars not reach for those with newer wounds? The community of the Cross first formed around a naked carpenter. It has no choice but to become a community of acceptance.

Lonely Living

Finally, the community of the Cross will always deal with our *aloneness*. "Strike the shepherd, and the sheep will be scattered," said the Lord (Zech. 13:7 NIV). At the Cross, Jesus' friends fled into the mists of self-protection. Treachery and betrayal are cruel actions that pain any who stand or die alone. All of us feel a threshold of loneliness. Even at a party in which we are most convivial, we can feel alone. The inmost part of ourselves is always separate and hidden. We are a part of what David Riesman years ago called the "lonely crowd."

Dying alone, however, is the real pain of Calvary. Dying alone is immensely harder than living alone. In every case when I've counseled someone whose spouse died suddenly while away on some errand, much of the weeping was because they felt pain over the lonely dying of their spouse. One of our hymns weeps, "Wounded and bleeding, for sinners pleading—Blind and unheeding—dying for me!"[1]

"Promise you'll be there when I am dying," an elderly man once begged me. Who can promise this? Yet I *could* promise that God in Christ, by example of Calvary, never lets anyone die alone. Further, it is the assumption of all members of the community that we who belong will not tolerate anyone's loneliness if we can help it.

Mega-Egos in Micro-Empires

In Jerusalem in April 1961 a thin, gray man, under armed surveillance, walked daily to a cage of bulletproof glass and slipped on a headpiece that made it possible for him to communicate with a courtroom outside the transparent enclosure. A battery of more than five hundred reporters listened intently to the proceedings of the trial of Adolf Eichmann.

But Jesus' trial in Jerusalem, probably in April of A.D. 27, was far more significant than Adolf Eichmann's. Long after the little Nazi-German, who met justice in the Israeli court, has been forgotten, the trial of A.D. 27 will be remembered. Here Pilate the judge and Jesus the defendant faced a sea of torches whose flaming pitch warmly scented the brisk night air. Light from the flickering torches cast amber shadows over angry faces. Our faces are there as well. Here and there among the crowd one could see faces crowned by phylacteries pronouncing them "men of God." This, I suppose, was the jury! Are we not there too?

Dwarfed by the majestic facade of the Fortress Antonia, Jesus and Pilate confronted each other. We, the would-be innocents, behold their confrontation. They represented two kingdoms, and the political kingdom appeared to be the dominant one. But as empires have come and gone, the real kingdom remains unchanged—this kingdom throughout the passing of empires is the community of the Cross.

We live in the age of the private "kingdom builder"! Nothing wrecks the goals of God's community like the privatization of our ambition. Our appetites for the material are only a small function of our micro-empires. So many among us are monarchs in miniature, and like Pilate, we question Jesus' right to kingship. We are willing to concede that Jesus is the King of the Jews. We are even willing to concede that Jesus is the King of most Gentiles. But when it comes to our own petty microcosms of existence, *we* must be king and not Jesus. At such moments, we often shrug off the counsel of our brothers and sisters. The community of God and its redeeming work in his world is scuttled in favor of our own private agenda.

Pilate's skepticism turned Jesus over to the custody of Herod, who seemed to possess a petty power that allowed him to judge but not to convict.

Wanna See a Neat Trick? Don't Ask Jesus!

Herod is a man of whom Luke says, "He desired to see a sign." Poor Herod! Did he not know that this same Jesus had refused to leap from the pinnacle of the temple in order to proclaim himself Messiah? Jesus never profaned the power of God by performing signs and miracles for a circus crowd. Herod sought a spectacular something. He loved spectacle! The Jews were always speaking of divided seas, flaming serpents, and fiery furnaces. Herod would have liked to see some such sign (Luke 23:8). Nevertheless, Jesus was certainly not the one to gratify Herod's inordinate desire for spectacle.

> THE SAVING WORK OF OUR SAVIOR CANNOT PROSPER WHILE HIS COMMUNITY WANDERS IN SEARCH OF SOMETHING GLITZY TO FILL ITS SHALLOW HEART.

Herod is legion in the churches of our day. Fields of suburban Christians migrate from congregation to congregation, propelled by a wanderlust for the greatest Christian show on earth. This ecclesiastical restlessness thwarts the holy work of God's saving community. The saving work of our Savior cannot prosper while his community wanders in search of something glitzy to fill its shallow heart. The reverbs and amps and colored spots of contemporary worship can come to focus on a plastic discipleship where shepherds replace their crooks of pastoral care with vaudeville hats and canes.

If Pilate teaches us doubt and vacillation, Herod teaches us to desire a spectacular sign. This damnable desire for dramatics has duped us—even drugged us—with a narcotic lure toward the theatrical rather than the submissive. To King Herod, Jesus did not seem to have the charismatic showmanship that a reformer and Messiah should possess. Jesus refused to perform even one small sign for Herod's entertainment. One celestial rabbit from one little messianic hat would have done it. But Jesus is no trickster. He came not to entertain but to redeem. Jesus does not offer us a spotlight and gold slippers; he offers us a crown of thorns and a bloody stake.

There are those in the community who seem to feel that there is no salvation without spectacle. Have we not heard them say, "I'll tell you, people just aren't saved like they used to be"? Why do they say this? Are not people still saved by repentance and faith? "Yes," they continue, "but now people don't weep when they are saved." It is indeed a blessing to any Christian to see someone so overwhelmed by the magnanimity of God's redemption that he or she cannot restrain tears. Yet it must be realized that a quiet experience with God is no less redeeming than a thunderous encounter. In some respects, we are little different from those of the first century who said, "Lord, show us a sign."

Herod could not see that the supernatural signs he desired would have completely eliminated his necessity for faith. For that which we can see plainly requires no faith. Herod missed the kingdom because of his wooden insensitivity. Let us beware such surface signs. There have been few Constantines who saw letters of flame in the sky. Yet there have been many Wesleys who have felt those imperceptible flames of faith strangely warm their hearts. Let us cry out for Wesley's Christ rather than Constantine's.

The Triumph That Outgrows Its Need for Spectacle

Yet we do hunger for God's direction in life. Because of that yearning, some seminary students may be struggling with all that is in them. Does the Lord want them to serve in their home state or across the sea? How easy it would be if the Lord gave them a clear signal: one ball of fire for this land and two balls of fire if he wished them to serve elsewhere—a "one if by land and two if by sea" sort of beacon. But, as Jesus said to the sign-mongering apostles who were unable to heal a demoniac, there are certain things that come only by prayer and fasting. This is the way the apostles found the will of God, and this is how we find it, too. We, the saving community, can talk to God and therefore have no need of signs. The wheel that rolled for Ezekiel by the river Chebar need not roll for us, for we can pray.

Belief is the antidote to Pilate's doubt and Herod's empty spirit of display. In Luke 23:55 there is a mention of the women who followed Christ all the way from Galilee. How important it is for Jesus to have followers! Christianity only exists as long as Jesus has followers; when there are no followers, there is no kingdom community. The late Charles Malik, outstanding Lebanese statesman, implied that communism advanced because there are too few followers of Jesus. A past president of the General Assembly of the United Nations (1958), he said that Christendom can be preserved only if we return to Christ and follow him:

> In Christianity, God became man: think of the great honor to us weak men! Indeed, if you ask yourself honestly what it is that you wish to preserve in "our way of life," you will find that the things you value most are based squarely on the bedrock of religion. Honor. Duty. Justice. Freedom. Tolerance. Charity. Sharing. Repentance. These are also Christian concepts. Does it not follow, then, that if we are to preserve them, we must return to Christ as our Lord and Savior, and therefore as the guide for everyday living?[2]

If Christianity is to be preserved, we must follow Jesus. He must ever stand at the center of our community.

Resolved: I Will Be Owned by Him Who Owned Nothing

It is in *following* Christ that our Christianity becomes real. Groups do not follow Christ; individuals do. It is not "they" or "we" who follow, but "I." The kingdom of God is never a pluralized call. We each embrace it alone or not at all. It is said that the Galileans followed, but they followed individually. Regardless of what the rest of the community does, each of us must singularly follow Christ. We need to adopt for ourselves the resolution of Jonathan Edwards:

> Resolved: that every man should live to the glory of God.
>
> Resolved Second: That whether others do this or not, I will.[3]

Let us endeavor to follow Christ exactly as did the Galilean women in Luke 23. They are the real heroines of that chapter. They did not question Jesus' right to be King! They were not bound to him because they sought a sign! They followed him because of love. All they held in life was bound up in this man Jesus. When he breathed out his last on Golgotha, something vital in their breasts shriveled into nonexistence. Yet they are our teachers.

THE KINGDOM OF GOD IS NEVER A PLURALIZED CALL. WE EACH EMBRACE IT ALONE OR NOT AT ALL.

These women had followed from Galilee. It is such a long way from Galilee to Calvary. Maybe not in miles or fur- longs or kilometers, but it is a long way. Between Galilee and Calvary there were tears, humiliation, heartbreak, and "the thousand natural shocks that flesh is heir to."[4] Somewhere between the two, the kingdom of God splintered and fragmented into little groups of fearful believers. For the women who followed, God died between Galilee and Calvary. But they followed! Who were these women? They were part of that small but growing community of the Cross.

What a tribute is paid to those Galilean women who followed! Judas betrayed, but they followed! Peter denied, but they followed! Pilate questioned, but they followed! Even when all hope was gone, they followed to the very door of the tomb. Remarkable? Hardly! Let us not compliment them, for that is what the community is supposed to do. It is to follow! That's just normal "kingdom Christianity."

Once upon a tree there was a king! He died under the trilingual sign that proclaimed him *Rex, Basileus, Melek*— King! Let us own him as King and follow him, not as sign-mongers, but as subjects in need, accountable to each other in the community of the King!

Many follow Jesus
to the breaking of bread,
but few to the drinking
of the chalice
of his Passion.

Thomas à Kempis
THE IMITATION OF CHRIST

CHAPTER FIVE

The Tree of Treachery

WHEN WE ARE TRAITORS—WHEN WE ARE BETRAYED

Jesus answered, "It is the one to whom I will give this piece of bread when I have dipped it in the dish." Then, dipping the piece of bread, he gave it to Judas Iscariot, son of Simon. As soon as Judas took the bread, Satan entered into him. (John 13:26–27 NIV)

Now Judas, who betrayed him, knew the place, because Jesus had often met there with his disciples. (John 18:2 NIV)

"Et tu, Brute?" are the famous plaintive words of Shakespeare's Caesar to Brutus, who had just stabbed him. Who are the arch traitors in history and literature? For Othello, it is Iago; for Washington, Benedict Arnold; for Jesus, it is Judas. We, like these others who were betrayed, are ever surprised by the traitors who smile at us with offerings of friendship while they fondle concealed daggers to undo us. "How could you do this to me?" we cry in disappointment. We may try to protect our lost dignity by putting on an air of diffidence, but we are never quite the same again.

But the question "How could you do this to me?" smacks of both poor-little-me-ism and arrogance. Our question *should* be "Why not me?" If Jesus had to deal with treachery, why shouldn't I? Ronald Reagan and the pope were both shot by would-be assassins within the same period of time. The pope lamented, "How could they do this to me?" and the president said, "It must have been a democrat." I like

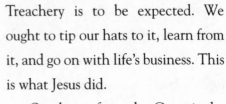

INTOLERANT OF THE JUDAS SYNDROME IN OTHERS, WE ARE BLIND TO IT IN OURSELVES.

the president's response best. Treachery is to be expected. We ought to tip our hats to it, learn from it, and go on with life's business. This is what Jesus did.

On the surface, the Cross is the result of one man's treachery. But Judas wears two faces: the face of a false lover and the face of a betraying confidant. I had several Judas archetypes in my mind. One of these comes from literature. Nathaniel Hawthorne's young goodman Brown comes upon a "black mass" in a New England wood one hapless night. As he passes, he sees the most revered Christians of the parish dancing naked in demonic ritual. He is not only shattered at that moment, but for the rest of his life his whole view of anyone he meets is tainted by what he doesn't know.

I'm not proud of it, but I have sometimes played the traitor. It is the nature of sinful humanity that we are all traitors, and yet oddly we despise the treachery beyond us. Intolerant of the Judas syndrome in others, we are blind to it in ourselves. In all honesty, treachery is probably the foundational transgression upon which all other sin is built. In one sense, it may be the original sin. Adam and Eve betrayed God in disobeying him, then in hiding the treachery of their half-eaten fruit.

Most of us are like Adam and Judas. Treachery is between us and those nearest to us. This should not surprise us, for in the strictest sense, only close friends can commit treachery. Those we barely know may be tyrants or ogres, but only a close friend can be treacherous.

Forgiving Treachery

Forgiving treachery may be duck soup for our grace-rich God, but it is likely the most difficult sin we ever ask others to forgive. I remember a poor woman who found out that her husband had been regularly committing adultery with his secretary. "He has betrayed me," she cried. "I will never, ever forgive him!"

A doctor of my acquaintance told me about his ruggedly handsome son who left seminary training to enter the gay community in Seattle. As if this was not heartbreaking enough for the physician, this same son fell in love and soon became engaged to an athlete. These successful young men openly announced their relationship and exchanged engagement rings. Their affair was ultimately consummated in engraved invitations and a very fashionable wedding, complete with cake and champagne. My doctor friend was at first shattered, but later consumed with hostility. However a more liberated world may feel about "sexual preferences," the doctor spoke of his own son's actions as a betrayal.

I and *you* are the pronouns of betrayal. "And you...Brutus—Judas...brother...friend." *I* is the dominant pronoun of the wounded ego. *I* got the dagger. *I* felt the blade. *I* was surprised. How could *you* do this to *me?*

While our turncoat friends catch us off guard, Judas's treachery did not surprise our Lord. He knew it was coming, and yet he set Judas free to do it. Judas seems predestined for the job, for he had "a devil" from the beginning (John 6:70–71). It is still to Jesus' great credit that he did not ask the disciples to physically coerce Judas into loyalty. I think it is remarkable that Jesus could free Judas from every requirement of personal loyalty. His example must be ours.

While we can never know who in our lives is a potential traitor, we must forever be setting our friends free from the necessity of being loyal. Only when we set them free can we be sure that their loyalty is spontaneous and uncoerced. Only then will their love be meaningful.

I often marvel that even in heaven, God allowed Lucifer his rebellion. God does not define time as we do. Still, I wonder how many minutes or millennia Lucifer lived loving God. Yet God allowed even him the freedom of his rebellion. Only when we permit our lovers the possibility of treachery does their faithfulness have any content!

Since Jesus knew what was in the heart of humanity, he was not surprised by treachery. He could live realistically. I do not advocate that we should be negative or live under some gloomy cloud of our own fashioning. I just think that human nature ought to be understood and that we ought never to gush in astonishment over anyone's treachery. All of us are capable of willfully acting in such strong self-interest that it must be interpreted as treachery by someone who trusts us.

Once upon a tree, the God-man was offered up at the hands of a friend turned traitor. But the outstanding teaching of the Cross is that it forgives all sin—treachery included. If Judas hanged himself and perished eternally, it is not because the Cross lacked the willingness to forgive him. It is that he never sought that forgiveness.

The Cross is the birthplace of forgiveness. Jesus was caught up in a project so huge that he would not distract himself with petty resentments. Yet he never whimpered, "How could he do this to me?" We do not hear him complain that Judas had done him dirty. Rather, he forges on with God's redeeming plan for his life. What excellence and wisdom there is in this!

It takes time to stop and avenge a traitor. I knew an old man once who bought his first automobile in the twenties.

It was one of those cars with open sides that allowed dogs to run up to the car and snap at the legs of motorists. But he paid these yapping predators little mind. "After all," he said, "if you stop to kick every dog that lunges at you, you never get anywhere in life." Jesus was too busy redeeming the world to take his precious time to "get even." The time we use in avenging ourselves is never time well spent.

A Cross above Self-Pity

To find God's plan for our lives is to crucify ourselves to all sniveling need for encouragement, or even counsel, when someone has injured us. When I remember that many without Christ are dependent on my faithfulness, I can sail through times of discouragement and betrayal without having to distract myself with self-pity.

THE TIME WE USE IN AVENGING OURSELVES IS NEVER TIME WELL SPENT.

How do I do this?

I believe there are two factors that bestow this spirit of largesse. First, there is the direct example of Jesus, which inspires my need to be like him—to act like him in the crisis. Needless to say, I live through difficulties in a positive manner when my emulation of Jesus derives directly from my continual conversation with him. In other words, I overcome the treachery of others by talking to Christ. Actually, it is not so much that I overcome my resentment of petty treachery. It's just that I am so pre-occupied with Jesus that I fail to notice it.

A second factor that contributes to this largesse is the indwelling Spirit of Christ. How so? Let us remember that the Spirit is interested in my submission to Jesus. Nearly all our littleness comes directly from self-concern. When we whimper, we are only serving our need to be stroked.

Often (but not often enough), I have felt the over-whelming presence of the Spirit draw me to a rapt hush. This state always focuses on the beauty and dignity of Christ. At such moments my resentment of others becomes impossible, for my relationship with Christ is my compelling concern.

Thursday's Wine

On that first Maundy Thursday, Jesus modeled the over-coming life. That first Gethsemane Thursday came as Thursdays always came. Nothing was different about it. A young rabbi, followed by a dozen husky men, sat down at a massive table, and a flagon of wine was emptied into a single cup. Each of the men had anticipated Thursday's party as a time of levity and warmth, but when the hour came, there was an unspoken dread in the air that choked lighthearted-ness. Yet in some ways it seemed to be an ordinary Thursday and, beyond it, only an ordinary Friday.

But nothing was ordinary.

A ghastly picture of Friday lay unseen on the surface of Thursday's wine. Ominously the portent floated on the deep-red liquid, framed by the oval rim of the metal chalice. There was a floating face on the surface of the wine. It was my face. I was still two thousand years away, yet my face was there, and my need for the bread and wine was there, too. But beside my face there floated a grim picture. What was this omen that lay unnoticed on the crimson-purple surface of the wine? It was the picture of a man with a hammer, who talked to himself as if he were lonely. I faced this hammer man one Easter as I wrote in my journal how he spoke to me in soundless words from the surface of the cup:

On with Friday's grisly business!
Let the broad arm raise the sledge!
Let the hammer ring out upon the nails.
I must not flinch when the crimson flows—
He's only a carpenter—
a craftsman who claimed too much.
"I need a black nail, soldier."
Give me your hand, carpenter.
What a strange man you are!
You stretch forth your hand too eagerly—
too willingly, as though I was going to shake it,
not nail it to a tree.
Steady, man. The first stroke of the hammer

is easiest for me and hardest for you.
For me the first blow meets only the resistance of soft flesh.
The hardwood beneath drives much slower.
For you the first blow is the worse.
It brings the ripping pain and the bright gore.
The wood beneath your wrist does not feel and bleed as you do.

Suddenly one of the Twelve must have jolted the table, and the ripples in the wine erased the unseen specter. Then the real drama began. The yet-unpierced hand reached for the cup. Thus our Christ began his dying work. I needed life, and so he lifted the cup. Friday was the day they raised up the cross, but Thursday was the day he faced and conquered death for me—all ahead of time. On Thursday, Christ raised the chalice and in a sense toasted the possibility of my soul.

I suspect that on Thursday he took a stance between me and his Father. To please his Father was to sacrifice himself for me. He knew his dying was necessitated by his one desire—to please his Father. And so who can deny that his dying was in Gethsemane, when he said, "Yes, Father"? In that resolve his life was already on the cross for my sake, although the actual bleeding would come later. Jesus had me in mind when he passed the wine to his friends. He served it to a dozen men with Aramaic names. But make no mistake about it: When he drank the cup of ages, he thought of me.

Even as he drank, Christ had no misgivings about the

coming day. He knew that somewhere in the city lay a cross, already hewn. In a few hours, that Thursday would be forever gone, and Jesus would be facing an ordeal that few men ever faced: a Roman crucifixion. He was tired, worn with the dread of it all, and needed rest for the brutal Friday. Still, there had to be one final attempt to explain to the disciples the essence of redemption.

As he lifted the cup he said to them, "This do in remembrance of me!" (1 Cor. 11:25 KJV). In effect, he was saying, "Remember tomorrow! For what shall happen tomorrow concerns everyone who ever shall live. God shall have nails in his hands tomorrow. God shall be scourged and mocked tomorrow. Tomorrow, I shall die. Remember tomorrow."

WITH HIS GRIM PREDICTIONS STILL IN THE AIR, EACH MAN SIPPED THE SIGN OF LIFE AND PASSED THE CUP TO THE NEXT.

The Latin base word for *communion* (to be one with) describes both my need and his intent. Our Savior, not yet wounded in his hands, drinks and passes the wine to me. I drink in my oneness with him, and all who will believe become my brothers and sisters in this common cup.

Dramatically Jesus had reached for Thursday's loaf. With almost sudden violence, he tore it in two. This is what he seemed to say, "Do you see this bread? Eat it! Tomorrow my body will be torn like this!" Then he breathed a prayer and lifted the cup and spoke the phrase whose larger meaning was: "My blood will flow as easily as this wine. Drink and remember tomorrow!"

One by one the men considered his chilling prophecies of the yet-unborn Friday. Silently the cup rose to the lips of a publican. Then a fisherman received the cup and drank of it and passed it to a zealot. Their eyes, glistening with sorrow, were fastened on the Master. With his grim predictions still in the air, each man sipped the sign of life and passed the cup to the next.

The Contagion of Melancholy

The contagion of the melancholy that had come over the Twelve kept conversation to a minimum as they left the upper room and hurried toward the park in the valley of the Kidron. Are we not there? Do we not rise—all ages—from that narrow table and once again join the millions of lovers who have lifted that sweet cup as members of his glorious, growing family? Do we not, the saved of all ages, hear Jesus say:

You will all fall from your faith; for it stands written:
"I will strike the shepherd down and the sheep will
be scattered."

...Peter answered, "Everyone else may fall away, but I will not."

Jesus said, "I tell you this: today, this very night, before the cock crows twice, you yourself will disown me three times."

But he insisted and repeated: "Even if I must die with you, I will never disown you."

And they all said the same. (Mark 14:27–31 NEB)

This is the tragedy of Thursday: Eleven men pledged themselves to commitments they would never keep. They were but the strong promises of weak men. We the weak still make strong promises. We need Christ—if for no other reason than we are all people of large professions and little deeds.

Judas, Brutus, and the Like

So Thursday became known as the day of apostolic treason and betrayal. The baleful treachery of Judas is Thursday's tale. Judas, the Benedict Arnold of the apostolate, the arch-Brutus of the early church, was a knight of the new kingdom. In spite of Matthew's experience with facts and figures, Judas had been ordained the keeper of the purse. He was the steward of the combined legacies of thirteen men. He dispersed the funds and was doubtless conscientious in the spending of all that had been committed to his keeping.

It may well have been Judas's dedication to faithful accounting that led him to look with disfavor on the King and his kingdom. For three years, Jesus had been speaking of a great kingdom. Perhaps an impatient Judas scorned the fact that after all that time this "great kingdom" still numbered only twelve subjects. Even so, it was no small task to manage the scant economies of thirteen men. Feeding them alone was a strain on the budget that must have kept Judas scratching his head and calculating expenses. To trim unnecessary spending, the group often lived out-of-doors, sleeping in open parks and gardens like the one in which the apostles were sleeping on the night of Jesus' arrest. Typical of all good treasurers, Judas probably resented all unnecessary spending and extravagant waste.

His resentment of all lavish waste may have been the very issue behind Thursday's bargain with the priests. Only four days before in nearby Bethany, Mary, the sister of the resurrected Lazarus, had done something that appeared to Judas a wasteful and extravagant sentiment (John 12:1–6). She had taken a pound of spikenard, a costly cosmetic, and poured it on Jesus' feet. Spikenard was a rare Himalayan flower, and many thousands of these precious blossoms had to be crushed to produce a pound of the fragrant oil. The ointment was so costly that the price of the one pound that Mary lavished on Jesus would have kept some poor family in food for a whole year.

The price of the spikenard would have doubtless gone a long way also in supporting an itinerant rabbi and his retinue. Judas explosively condemned the gift as waste: "Why was not this ointment sold for three hundred pence, and given to the poor?" (John 12:5 KJV). Nevertheless, Jesus defended Mary's deed and spoke with a curt finality that Judas could not possibly mistake: "Let her alone: against the day of my burying hath she kept this" (v. 7 KJV). It may have been that Judas felt a stinging repudiation in this and that his brooding, injured self-respect was the seedbed of Thursday's betrayal. Wounded pride often gives birth to vengeance.

Thirty pieces of silver was the contracted price. It was a pitiful sum whose current equivalent would be twenty-four dollars. Can this be the very Judas who objected to wasteful spending? Judas, this is such poor economics. Twenty-four dollars for silencing lips that uttered the Sermon on the Mount! Twenty-four pitiful dollars for the fastening of hands that broke the bread of redemption in the upper room! There is none who can excuse your betrayal, Judas! You well deserve to be called Satan's Saint!

God Slayer! Savior-killer!
Murderer of Mary's Son!
Butcher-fiend of Love and Grace!
Monster! Traitor! Evil One!

It is you, who raised his cross,
Stained his palms, and pierced his side.
Turncoat against the Son of God,
You had the Master crucified.
Whenever evil men loathe light,
And Hell seeks to include us,
Decent men will curse your name,
Darkened, Son of Satan, Judas![1]

There is an ugliness and loneliness in betrayal. It alienates the betrayer from the betrayed. So it was with Judas that Thursday night on the way to Gethsemane. He had bargained to lead the officials to the person of Jesus. Even though Judas was in the company of soldiers, a new loneliness was stealing into his life. It was that utter loneliness that never again found a friend.

The Kiss That Stood for Nothing

Judas walked with reluctance amidst the clanking of armor and the pungent odor of blazing pitch from a dozen torchfires. The soldiers' swords, which Judas was sure would not be needed, glistened in the starlight as the temple guards entered the garden. The sleeping, groggy apostles awoke. They were too stunned to run or fight. They watched through bleary eyes as Judas advanced to Jesus, kissed him, and said, "Hail, Master!"

The kiss was the signal of identification, and Christ was arrested.

This is the most famous kiss of recorded time. Yet it is history's greatest lie—the kiss that stood for nothing. Anyone who saw it might have reasoned, "My, how Judas loves the Master." Yet the kiss said something else. Jesus had nothing to fear from the soldiers and the priests. They were clearly his enemies. Jesus' declared enemies had never intimidated him. It was Iscariot alone, his lover in pretense, who was able to betray him. The greatest enemies of Christ have always been those who pretend to be his friends.

THE GREATEST ENEMIES OF CHRIST HAVE ALWAYS BEEN THOSE WHO PRETEND TO BE HIS FRIENDS.

Judas was the ancestor of all who wear the double mask of allegiance and treason. Many who would scorn Judas's betrayal for thirty pieces of silver betray Christ daily for less. We, the pretended lovers of Christ, still throng today's churches and fall asleep in Gethsemane. The Judas kiss has become so common that even our sincere love for Christ is often called suspect. In any present list of disciples, the traitors seem to outnumber the true. Judas's treachery still makes many crosses in today's churches. It fabricates them out of gossip and half-truths and then hangs the reputations of good men on the betrayals of the double-minded. Betrayal always trespasses against love and confidence. We are saved eternally but only temporarily loyal. We say, "Lord, Lord," but do not the things he says (Luke 6:46).

As was the case of Judas and Jesus, so it always is. A pastor of my acquaintance had given his secretary his utter trust and confidence. She betrayed his trust. Never openly, mind you, for a Judas never makes his bargains in the sunlight. She did it by leaving question marks in her statements about her pastor, being sure that her every comment about him had some double meaning. Her telephone calls from the church office were always full of "innocent" inflections that packed insinuations into her truth—which she "always" spoke. Her treachery so hacked at the pastor's respect that he left the church. This is the way the Judas sin nibbles at love and trust. The traitor forever appears to be a person of peace, full of friendly kisses in Gethsemane.

Betrayal inevitably ushers in that empty question about the worth and meaning of friendship. I believe that tears of disappointed love were swimming in Jesus' eyes as he voiced his heartache: "Judas, would you betray the Son of Man with a kiss?" (Luke 22:48). To those of us who harbor Judas in our hearts, he surely says, "Drive a dagger in my heart if you must, but don't preface it with pretense." We must not acquit ourselves by blaming Gethsemane on Judas. Our current treachery still hurts our current Lord.

At the beginning of this chapter we heard Shakespeare's dying Caesar say to the conspirator he thought to be his friend, "And you, Brutus?" In the same tender tone, Jesus said, "And you, Judas?"

Judas Day

The Judas-life does not always end in suicide, but it always ends empty and hungry. Beyond Gethsemane there was nothing left for Judas but a gnarled, twisted tree on a canyon rim. There, from a knotted limb, hung a heavy rope; and in the chafing noose of its braided hemp hung the head of a faithless follower. Who knows whether in that last moment of life, he breathed again the treacherous formula, "Hail, Master."

Do not feel that Judas died an unusual death. All betrayal contains the seeds of self-destruction. Our own treacheries may not result in suicide, but they do kill our usefulness to God; they crucify our devotion to Christ. And while we may have breath and pulse, the true and uncreated Christ-life will still be missing in us. Somewhere on the backside of every cross is a hangman's tree. Each time we betray Christ, we stab at our own existence.

Thursday was Judas Day! It stood for betrayal, but it also stood for broken commitment. We have already seen how Simon Peter, on the way to the garden, pledged to stand by

Jesus, whatever might come. What magnificent promises he made. Oh, if only he had stood by those vows! "To prison and to death, but never to deny you," vowed Simon (Luke 22:33). So promised all the disciples.

Had the disciples lived out their promises, there may have been twelve crosses silhouetted against the Judean sky the very next day. Had they been the men they claimed to be on Thursday, Friday might have seen every one of them flogged and crowned with thorns. There could have been such blessed fellowship in their sufferings. They might have sung the rightness of their cause in a great chorus, from a dozen gallows. Together in death they might have linked nail-scarred hands and entered into glory— the faithful company of the ever faithful crucified lovers of Christ.

All the loyal promises of his twelve life-pledging friends went unfulfilled. The disciples vanished when the conflict came. They all fled, except for the youngest, John. How Christ must have leaned on that young man. He must have felt his silent strength in the judgment hall. He saw John's eyes study the stone floor when his clothing was stripped away. He loved the man whose cheeks glistened silver with tears when his Master was stretched to the whipping post. How much it must have meant to Jesus to look down from Friday's stake and see John standing at his feet, recklessly and courageously declaring himself the friend of a blasphemer. None of the other disciples stuck with him to declare their love.

I Pledge Allegiance to the Cross

Where were all those gallant men who declared their Thursday "Pledge of Allegiance"? Had they not dramatically sliced the air with great gestures of loyalty? One who had been the loudest with his promises warmed himself by a little courtyard fire that blazed outside the judgment hall. Simon Peter was possessed of that half-devotion maintained by so many modern disciples. He loved Jesus too much to utterly forsake him but not enough to go with him all the way to judgment. He vacillated between leaving altogether and going on into the judgment hall with John. Peter Marshall described Peter's serious but unstudied devotion in one of his prayers: "We are too Christian really to enjoy sinning, and too fond of sinning really to enjoy Christianity."[2]

The chill of the crisp night air may have prompted Peter to move closer to the fire, where others had gathered for warmth and conversation. The topic of conversation seemed to be the strange nocturnal proceedings of the trial then underway. Peter's mind ran feverishly over the fireside chatter, but his face registered little. The tongues of light that danced on glowing sticks in the courtyard fire suddenly brought Peter's face into full illumination so that a young woman in the group, with startling suddenness, lifted her finger toward Peter and said, "This man was also with him." Only the deep bronze tone of the old sailor's leathery complexion kept the hot blood from showing as it rushed to his face, and he blurted out the denial, "Woman, I know him not!" This little treachery put its tiny foot in the door of his heart and beckoned his full-grown betrayal to enter.

Instinctively, Peter drew back from the direct light of the flames. He pulled his hood a little further forward on his forehead. Those titan hands, made strong by tugging soggy nets, trembled like the infirm fingers of an old man. But the shadows were not deep enough to hide him. A bystander, who perhaps had heard

> THIS LITTLE TREACHERY PUT ITS TINY FOOT IN THE DOOR OF HIS HEART AND BECKONED HIS FULL-GROWN BETRAYAL TO ENTER.

Jesus teach and was sure that Peter was with him, affirmed what the girl had said: "You are one of them." With a tinge of anger at the charge of being disciple to an accused blasphemer, Peter answered hotly, "Man, I am not!" (Luke 22:58 NIV).

The accusations subsided—temporarily.

Time dragged on.

Inside the hall, Christ was being victimized by cankered

justice and false witnesses. Outside, Peter was the victim of his own shabby dedication and a trio of accusers. After an hour had passed, a third man, who'd been sitting by the fireside and studying Peter's Galilean brogue, made an abrupt accusation: "Surely you are one of them, for your accent gives you away" (Matt. 26:73 NIV). A fit of temper seized the big apostle, and in anger he swore and cursed his accusers. His rage burned over the stigma of his friendship with Christ.

Imagine this great hulk of a man gone out of control. One of his hands closes on the clothing of his accuser. The other clenches into a fist, which he brandishes like a weapon in the air above the poor man's head as he shouts with white-hot profanity, "I know not the man!" Startled by his violence, all eyes in the little enclosure fall instantly on Peter. Shocked into dumbness, no one speaks.

The piercing scream of a cock shatters the still night air. Its shrill cry, like the unsteady note of a trumpet, calls to mind Peter's Thursday promise. He releases his trembling accuser as tears come with stinging suddenness to his eyes. He buries his head in his huge hands and sobs his way out of the plaza. He has been unfaithful to his Lord. Thursday meant nothing. He has done nothing he promised. His Lord would soon be on a cross, and Jesus' loneliness would be the unspeakable result of Peter's treachery.

I have emulated "Saint" Peter. His unsaintly soul so

resembles mine. I promise Christ allegiance and give him denial. Then, broken, I cry my way into his presence.

Dear Christ,
Look not from Pilate's whipping tree
For there you will but gaze on me.
Congeal the faithless blood that ought to flow
Each time I hear the cock's condemning crow.[3]

Once I have known the exhilaration of love committed unto Christ, I must guard myself lest there come to me some bitter night of denial and betrayal. But are we not all alike on Maundy Thursday? Somewhere in the process of undedicated living, by a thoughtless deed we may forget all we have affirmed. Is our commitment to the Master authentic? We must examine it. Try it. Prove it. We who have promised Christ all must cherish the very Cross that makes us so afraid. Only as we conquer our Cross-fear enough to embrace it and claim it as our own can we call ourselves his friends.

If you will be My disciple,

deny yourself.

If you will possess the pleased life,

despise this present life.

If you will be exalted in heaven,

humble yourself in this world.

If you will reign with Me,

bear the cross with Me.

Thomas à Kempis

THE IMITATION OF CHRIST

CHAPTER SIX

The Culprits of the Cross

ANSWERING OUR OWN ACCOUNTABILITY

When Pilate saw that he was getting nowhere, but that instead an uproar was starting, he took water and washed his hands in front of the crowd. "I am innocent of this man's blood," he said. "It is your responsibility!" (Matt. 27:24 NIV)

We did it. The crucifixion. We did it! We decent people. We the sophisticated. We the successful. We raised the cross. The debt, the crime, the need for it—it's all ours. And now we must answer the issues: "How was it that first Good Friday?" "What are the names of those who caused the Cross?"

A Dying Time for Three

Once upon a tree, the Savior of the world died at the hands of those he came to save. With him died two criminals—these convicts knew not the Savior nor what his death would mean. Three naked men they were—stumbling to their gallows. Let us squint our eyes and summon our hearts to behold the unfolding executions of the day.

There is an expression of terror on the face of the first

bandit. With a sobriety born of fear, he watches the soldiers prepare his torture. His reasoning is muddled. His mind examines his condemnation. The sight of a huge man with a hammer leering at him shoots an icicle into his trembling frame. Then his thoughts are abruptly interrupted when the soldiers come to fasten him to his tree. He struggles against them. His leg lashes out and sends one of the soldiers sprawling into the dirt. His hands clench into fists and flail at chests protected by bronze armor. He spits in their faces and curses them and the laws of their state. But soon his execution is underway, and he is securely fastened to his instrument of death. When the first pains begin to rack his body, his thirst-crazed lips part and issue a scream of horror that cause all who hear it to shrivel inwardly.

The second bandit's thoughts are little different from the first's. Perhaps he has reasoned that what will be, will be, so he does not fight against the executioners—there is simply no use. He is determined to be brave in his demeanor and to take his impending torturous death "like a man." He has managed to raise a little courage in his faint heart. He does quite well until that hellish moment the first man loses his self-control and screams. It is that scream, like the howl of a desperate animal caught in the jaws of a steel trap, that steals his bravado. Instantly he feels himself go limp.

He studies the gallows on which his pitiful friend is hanging. Perspiration pops out in little drops of anguish all over his brow as he watches the soldiers make ready his own death. The frozen air seems to chill him, as he shudders convulsively. Then the soldiers come. His resolve melts, he struggles violently. In one Herculean spasm of energy, he almost kicks himself free, but soon he, too, is dying. He bites his lip to fight back the scream of terror that threatens to erupt from his mouth.

There is a third man yet to die—Jesus of Nazareth. But this man is clearly no thief. It is as though he has for years studied the prospect of dying this horrible death and is utterly resigned to it. He is not possessed by the panic and fear of the other two. The soldiers do not have to drag Jesus to his death. A king must die as a king. When his time comes, he walks resolutely to his cross and lies down upon it.

Then, with an eerie willingness, he stretches out his left hand to the executioner. A black nail is placed at his wrist. The hammer man hesitates momentarily, and Jesus looks at him as if to say, "Suffer it to be so now, for so it must be to fulfill all righteousness!" And with that look of reassurance, the hammer falls on the spike with repeated

WITH AN EERIE WILLINGNESS, HE STRETCHES OUT HIS LEFT HAND TO THE EXECUTIONER.

blows until the hand is secured to the cross. Then this confident Nazarene stretches out his right hand and looks again into the eyes of the mallet man as if to say, "If a man shall spike thy left hand to the cross, offer to him thy right hand also." Soon that hand, too, is fastened. Then the ugly stake is raised. The cross is wedged into the earth.

Boldly silhouetted against the dawn that ugly April morning stood Earth's greatest symbol of love. People asked what it meant then. We are still asking what it means today. The Cross is problematic because it defies human logic and reason. Its eternal intricacies escaped even the analysis of thinkers like Anselm and Aquinas. How can we smaller minds ever apprehend its glory?

Yet the Cross is central in Judeo-Christian history. All that precedes it is preparation. All that comes after it is consequence. It has become the theme of countless volumes, the subject of artistic masterpieces, the object of theological controversies. No one who believes in Christ and his gospel can get along without the Cross. It is the reason anyone ever comes to believe in the first place. For at the Cross the founder of Christian faith and all later defenders of that faith are introduced. Every virtue of Christianity is present in the Cross. Every sin is also there. In this strange mix, we can see that the Cross is where Christ's virtue answers our sin. At Calvary, God perfected the art of dying till it covered the crime of artless living.

If We Would Know Love

I stand beneath the glaring light of "why?" I gaze at bloody wood and my "why" is answered by a great cry from heaven, "Sin is why—your sin. Sin has one great remedy—love!"

Then I see it—love—real, selfless love—I am the focus of God's almighty love. The Cross is heaven's bloody, costly Valentine. And I see not only that God loves, but how much he loves. Sacrifice lies beneath his enigmatic tree of death. So does forgiveness. Righteousness? Yes, it is there in abundance. Having studied the tree, perhaps I will gain an energized spirit of my own transformation. I gaze at it and sing.

> *Years I spent in vanity and pride,*
> *Caring not my Lord was crucified,*
> *Knowing not it was for me He died*
> *On Calvary.*[1]

Now I know that the Cross is not an impersonal symbol, swept away by decades of lawless, unorganized time. It is never this. The Cross is for me! It is personal! It is personal because it is my greatest need.

The Cross confers on me the glorious attribute of belonging. It belonged to Jesus. It belonged to him long before the eighteenth year of Tiberius, the year in which he died. It was his long before the tree from which it was made

113

was even a sapling. It belonged to him before the cosmos was framed. Long before God ever spangled the black canvas of night with a thousand glittering constellations, the Cross belonged to Jesus.

And in the dim ages while God awaited my brief lifetime, the Cross was already waiting, like a wooden savior to rescue me when the time came. Christ would meet me at the stake when I was in need of the serpent on the pole. If I would but look, I could live. God, who sits above the ages and sees the past, present, and future at a single glance, had his saving grace stacked up in the future storehouse of my need.

> CHRIST WOULD MEET ME AT THE STAKE WHEN I WAS IN NEED OF THE SERPENT ON THE POLE. IF I WOULD BUT LOOK, I COULD LIVE.

I thrill that God would so lavishly spend his best for me. Christ looked upon my pain and purchased my healing with nails and ropes and thorns. The pain most severe to the Master may have been the anguish of my fickle and frequent doubt and unbelief. The hurts I often bring him cannot be assuaged with balms or diminished by narcotics. No, they require his very blood.

It seems to me my fickle faith must cause him to ask me, as he asked his Father, "Hast thou forsaken me [too]?"

The Cross Bequeathed

The Cross belonged to Jesus so that he could bequeath it to me. What belonged to the Teacher was to belong to me. In fact, Jesus taught that unless I own the Cross, I cannot be his disciple: "And anyone who does not carry his cross and follow me cannot be my disciple" (Luke 14:27 NIV). Cross-bearing is to stand at the imperative center of my discipleship.

My baptismal certificate can tell me that I have been baptized. A form letter tells me that I am a church member. But only a cross borne on my back tells me that I am a disciple. No cross...no claim of belonging to God.

We have developed some strange concepts as to what cross-bearing really means. What did Jesus mean when he said that we should take up a cross? He was not referring to a dainty trinket dangling from a gold chain. Neither was he referring to a silver and ebony crucifix suspended at the end of a rosary. Nor did he mean a grand cathedral cross carried in the processional of the Eucharist.

Our cross is something vital we endure for the Lord of the kingdom. For Stephen, it was martyrdom. For Paul, it meant making his own defense before Nero. For Dietrich Bonhoeffer, it meant being hanged by the Nazis. For Jim Elliot, it was an inspired attempt to draw God's circle of love around savage tribesmen. For William Wallace, it was death in a communist prison cell.

115

I can see that it is wrong to refer to the trivial things of my life as "my cross." That which I give up for Lent is not my cross. A toothache is not my cross. The lack of some particular talent that would add energy or charm to my personality is not my cross. Before I hastily designate anything as "my cross," I must ask myself what a cross really is. I must look at *his* Cross and then ask myself what I have offered him by way of sacrifice, humility, and obedience.

I must free myself from that mistaken notion that a cross belongs in the front of a church. Crosses belong on the backs of Christians. Remember how happy Christian was in Bunyan's *The Pilgrim's Progress* when he finally came to the Cross? He came to the Cross, and it felt wonderful! For the first time that he could remember, he could walk straight. The sins of a lifetime had bent him until life was burdensome. When he faced the Cross of Christ, the burdens rolled off his back and on down the path into the empty tomb. He straightened up and walked away with a sprightly step. There was a new light and free energy about him. Christian's heavy load of guilt was all taken away at the Cross.

Soon he discovered, however, that God had taken the sin from his back only to replace it with a cross. The Cross does not free me from sin so that I can live any way I wish and participate in any activity whatsoever. No, the Cross removes the burdens of guilt I carry so that I can be free to bear the Cross of Christ on my own back.

The kingdom of God has no citizens who are not cross-bearers. We must own the Cross! How does the Cross of Christ become ours? By openly admitting that we are involved with Jesus. We cannot share his triumph without sharing in his responsibility. We will never carry the Cross of Christ unless somehow we become convinced that the cross on which Jesus died is the outcome of *our* sin.

Jesus' untimely death was not just to deal with the sin of those who were his contemporaries. The crucifixion was God's dramatic answer to the sins of all humanity. The Cross was raised in the sands of the first century, but its shadow falls the entire length of calendar time. The Cross was lifted up to deal with the sins of Simon Peter, Augustine, Martin Luther, John Wesley, and it was lifted up to deal with my sins too. I cannot push the responsibility of the Cross onto Pilate or Herod or Roman legionaries or Jewish priests. It is my deliverance, and it is my crime! One Good Friday I wrote these lines:

> *"Not my sin, oh Lord," I cried,*
> *"that murdered God.*
> *At Calvary the star of distant heaven*
> *bled—but not for my iniquity."*

Christ said, "My son, the crime of time
is your own felony.
For you the hate of planet Earth
fell heavy on me.
It was because you needed life,
My life was counted loss.
I was suspended from the tree
and life dripped from my cross.
And, although ebbing centuries
have passed away since then,
you share this human homicide
and need the world's Friend."

Interesting to Many; Vital Only to a Few

The Cross is still relevant, even in an age when we hurl new stars into the night and program interplanetary travel. It is still the only hope of individuals, even in this noonday of human intellect and achievement. But it seems not to impress many in our age. It has numerous pretenders, but few defenders. This is no surprise to the disciples of Christ; for Jesus taught that the Cross would be interesting to the masses, but vital to only a few. He predicted that many would be called, but few would be chosen (Matt. 22:14).

Countless people have seen the Cross, but few carry it. Some time ago, I went to see one of those "biblical" movies. Just before the intermission, the crucifixion was presented in breathtaking color and drama. The sounds of the hammer, ringing out upon the nails, echoed through the stereophonic speaker system of the theater; it was a frigid sort of clang that sent a shiver through the audience. Then the cross was lifted upright in the center of the wide screen. Behind the cross, the wide-angle camera swept the heavens.

JESUS TAUGHT THAT THE CROSS WOULD BE INTERESTING TO THE MASSES, BUT VITAL TO ONLY A FEW.

Then the celluloid film projected a dark carbon incandescence, and the screen boiled with angry clouds made dark and heavy by rain. The soundtrack ricocheted the roll of ear-splitting thunder. After a raucous, sudden clap of thunder, the camera fell once more on the cross. Blood was beginning to run from the wound in one of Christ's hands. It ran red and vivid and bright on the dull, rough, brown wood and dripped over the crossbeam in a tiny rivulet. In the center of the cross, it was joined by another little stream, running from the wound in his other hand. That tiny ribbon of red continued down the vertical wooden beam and began collecting in a depression at the foot of the cross.

Then the rain began to fall. It accumulated in that small basin and mingled with the red. Soon the pool filled to overflowing and began trickling down the mountainside. The small red rill combined with other torrents of rushing water. Finally it became a great crimson tide for this world's salvation—but, more that that, for *my* salvation.

It was magnificent. I was thunderstruck with the majesty and the horror of Calvary. What a commanding portrayal of the pageant of redemption. Then, before I was ready to leave the scene, the film sequence stopped. The lights slowly illuminated the theater and filled it with a pale twilight.

It took a moment or so for me to make the trip from Calvary back to the theater. But soon I found myself in the aisle, elbow to elbow with others in the audience, making my way to the lobby. I wondered if everyone had been as awestruck with the Cross as I had been.

In the lobby, men laughed and chattered as though nothing had happened. Jewelry-bedecked women tossed their heads with lighthearted caprice. Children clamored for a drink at the water fountain. A noisy line formed at the concession booth. In the lounges, theater-goers used language that suggested the very antithesis of what they had just witnessed.

Most people who see the Cross are not impressed with it. They can see it and walk away and forget it. Yet real

Christians see the Cross and esteem it. Such disciples of Christ understand their debt. The Cross is theirs.

Buying a One-Way Ticket to Forever

Our debt is his sacrifice; his sacrifice is our debt. How far does our obligation reach?

Paul seemed to believe that once we understand the price that Jesus paid to set us free, we truly are in debt. "Therefore, brothers, we have an obligation," he said (Rom. 8:12 NIV), and the obligation stems from his gift of salvation that was purchased at the Cross. "I am obligated both to Greeks and non-Greeks, both to the wise and the foolish," said the apostle (Rom 1:14 NIV). It is never enough to accept the finished work of Christ and spend the currency of his forgiveness totally on ourselves. The burden to share the Cross and its message lay so hard upon Paul that he cried, "Woe be unto me if I preach not the gospel!" (1 Cor. 9:16). Surely this wonderful salvation we own is not ours to hide and protect. It is given to us to share until all the world we touch is as free as we are.

Arthur Blessitt once devoted his life to carrying a physical cross around the world. He dragged it across the continents—from Africa to Asia, from Europe to North and South America. When I first learned of his devotion to the idea, I felt that he was a sensationalist and that sooner or later his reputation would be rendered bogus. But after seeing all his years of dedication to the project, I now believe that Arthur understood that he was obligated to portray this unforgettable image of discipleship.

Through the Sahara, across Arabia, through the jungles, and along the steppes, through rain or sunshine and into the vast arenas where athletes compete, Arthur and his cross could be seen. His was a debt that owned him. His Christ could not be shunted aside while Arthur merely lived as most of us do—going our separate ways, making a living, or (as in my case) writing books about our fever for the issue.

I only hope that the image of Arthur Blessitt's discipleship may settle into my consciousness until I freely admit that I, too, am a debtor. Once I totally acknowledge my debt, perhaps I will begin to repay it by offering myself to Jesus more completely. Then shall my life sing with Sir John Bowring:

> *In the Cross of Christ I glory,*
> *Tow'ring o'er the wrecks of time;*
> *All the light of sacred story*
> *Gathers round its head sublime.*[1]

The hope which was
then entertained scarcely
by one thief on the cross is
now cherished by nations
everywhere on earth, who are
marked with the sign of the
cross on which he died that
they may not die eternally.

Augustine
THE CITY OF GOD

CHAPTER SEVEN

The Death of Death

AFRAID OF NEITHER DEATH NOR DYING

And when Jesus had cried out again in a loud voice, he gave up his spirit. At that moment the curtain of the temple was torn in two from top to bottom. The earth shook and the rocks split. The tombs broke open and the bodies of many holy people who had died were raised to life. They came out of the tombs, and after Jesus' resurrection they went into the holy city and appeared to many people. (Matt. 27:50–53 NIV)

"To die well is to die willingly," wrote Seneca. And so when I think of Christ at his execution, I must remember again that he said, "I lay down my life...and no man takes it from me" (John 10:17–18). Is it possible that he anticipated his own death? Was he not but thirty-three years old and in love with his Father's world? He was, and yet I believe that he did anticipate death. He knew he was born to die and that his dying was of such monumental importance that his living would have to accommodate the full knowledge of how his life would end. But with cheer? Yes, to some degree. The joy of his sacrifice came in knowing it was his Father's will and therefore it was his passion.

A Truce before Dying

Still he knew the task would not be easy. The very thought of dying made the Master sweat great drops of blood in Gethsemane (Luke 22:44). There come those times of final pain when we would gladly make a truce with death. Such times come with agony. The Cross becomes the prime example of all that dying may require. Dying comes in all varieties. Some dying does not leave us until it has killed our dignity. Long and gradual dying steals all the sparkle from a gallant passing. We may at last end up a skin-and-bones replica of the real person God created us to be. Musetta Gilman wrote on the death of her friend:

> I never thought that I
> Would make a truce with you,
> Oh, Death—
> Waxer of faces;
> Stealer of breath.
> But when I saw her bones
> Securely bound in linkless chain
> Victim of torture;
> Prisoner of pain;
> Her brilliant mind divorced
> From sight, from sound
> No longer free.

Stalker at midnight,
Keeper of key,
You loosened her bond
Restored dignity.[1]

Yet it is not with death that we would seek a truce, but with dying. For most of us fear not the state of death; it is the final passage that leads to it that we most fear. Yet, how well Christ lives out the doctrine of Seneca—dying both willingly and well.

But of what personal and individual significance is the crucifixion of one single, Nazarene rabbi? Why does the untimely death of this young and gentle Jesus have more meaning than the death of any other great man? Why should we regard him any more highly than Socrates, who obediently drank his hemlock? What deed of his is more praiseworthy than that of Joan of Arc, who humbly committed herself unto God from a flaming stake? Has his life been more fruitful or his death more grieved than India's courageous Gandhi?

> LONG AND GRADUAL DYING STEALS ALL THE SPARKLE FROM A GALLANT PASSING.

Let us say simply that the Cross stands for death. To be sure, it is a more dramatic kind of death than most people ever experience. Still, it is not the most horrible death ever endured. In fact, Jesus' crucifixion itself is not unique. One has only to observe the biographies of Antiochus the Seleucid or Nero the Emperor to see how very common crucifixions once were. Thousands of such executions came before the Cross of Christ, and thousands followed it.

Reusing Old Gallows

It even seems likely that Jesus was not the first person to die on the very cross that took his life. Crosses were gallows of execution and were probably used over and over again. Perhaps his very cross had been stained with the blood of a score of corpses before Jesus died there. Doubtless it was used for other executions after his own. It would have been as unthinkable to use a cross only once as it would have been for French "citizens" to use a guillotine only once or for a state penitentiary to use an electrocution device for only one condemned prisoner. Suffice it to say, Jesus' suffering was neither unique nor inordinately longer than others'. Even the thieves who died beside him suffered longer than he did.

If all these things are true concerning the Cross, why has the Cross become the ensign and standard of Christianity? Remember, the Cross stands for DEATH. It really represents two sorts of death: the death of a particular man named Jesus, and the principle of death as it relates to all of us. In short, his death and ours.

Death: Not the Terror We Supposed

Death and dying have become a kind of preoccupation for the West. People who "have everything" think about death incessantly and try to analyze the concept. There was a day when we all spoke openly about death and guardedly of sex. Now we have somewhat reversed the tone and frequency of our conversations. Although we realize the reality of death, we speak of it in hushed tones and euphemisms—and that only when we absolutely must.

But the Cross teaches us that death is not the terror we supposed. Jesus, dying in the most excruciating way, was not dead for long. In the chronicles of God, no death has ever lasted long. We fall asleep on this cruel planet and wake up a world away. It is amazing just how often the New Testament speaks of death as sleep (Acts 7:60; 1 Cor. 11:30; 15:51; 1 Thess. 4:14). John Chrysostom in the fourth century said,

> *What is death at most?*
> *It is a journey for a season:*
> *a sleep longer than usual.*
> *If thou fearest death,*
> *thou shouldst also fear sleep.*[2]

Death is not only sleep; it is a sleep of transformation. Paul said, "We will not all sleep [or die], but we will all be changed" (1 Cor. 15:51 NIV). We all look forward to sleeping this wonderful sleep of transformation. Ben Franklin wrote this epitaph for his own gravestone:

The body of
Benjamin Franklin, Printer,
Like the cover of an old book,
Its contents torn out,
And stript of its lettering and gilding,
Lies here, food for worms;
But the work shall not be lost,
For it will, as he believ'd,
Appear once more
In a new and more elegant edition,
Corrected and improved
By the Author.[3]

Jesus' own body was changed into a more transcendent body just by dying and receiving the Resurrection nature. He became the model of how death shall transform us as well: "For the trumpet will sound, the dead will be raised imperishable, and we will be changed. For the perishable must clothe itself with the imperishable, and the mortal with immortality" (1 Cor. 15:52–53 NIV). The Cross is really a golden lectern from which the world's greatest teacher gave us lessons in how to take the final and most difficult step of our physical lives.

Death: The Ultimate Statistic

Once upon a tree, the Son of God died. And God stood the Cross up to remind us that death is the inevitable end of every physical life. The Cross is singular evidence that even good men die. I once read about a good man who was told by his physician that he had an incurable malignancy and was going to die. He would not die at that moment, or perhaps not even that month, but he would die. In his body he carried the sentence of death. The man was neither startled nor alarmed by the pronouncement. He knew that he could have said to the doctor who had issued the ultimatum, "You will die, too, Doc!" or he might have said to the whole planet, "You, too, will die, world!" Death is the great inevitable statistic, cried George Bernard Shaw—one out of one must die.

There is an ancient fable of Baghdad that tells of a merchant who sent his servant to the bazaar to purchase food. After only a few minutes, his servant came back and fell at his employer's feet. Pale with fear, he begged, "A horse, a swift horse, please, master. Down at the market I bumped into a woman, and when she turned around and faced me I could see that the woman was Death. She raised her arm to strike me, but I escaped her. Please, I must have a horse— your fastest. I will escape Death by riding to Samarra."

The merchant loaned his slave his fastest horse and went to the bazaar, where he, too, saw Death standing among the shambles. "Why did you terrorize my servant this morning?" the merchant asked Death.

"I didn't mean to terrorize your servant. Mine was only a reaction of surprise. I was astonished to see him here in Baghdad, for I have an appointment with him tonight in Samarra."[4]

DEATH, INDEED, IS THAT LAND FROM WHICH NO TRAVELER RETURNS.

Death, indeed, is that land from which no traveler returns. We all must die. "It is appointed unto men once to die," say the Scriptures (Heb. 9:27 KJV). Nothing can prevent it!

The idea of ultimate and universal death is not just theological chitchat. C. G. Jung said it is our singular preoccupation after we reach the age of thirty-five. Biologists teach us that in all living organisms two principles exist: anabolism, the building of protoplasm; and catabolism, the breakdown of protoplasm. When the former exceeds the latter, there is growth. When the two are held in balance, there is stabilization. But when catabolism begins to occur at a faster rate, there is gradual disintegration and death. In short, from the very moment of conception, our own death is inherently part of our passing physiology.

Death is not a monster created by power-mad theological Frankensteins to scare unthinking individuals around to their viewpoint. Death is fact! It is a fact more unpleasant than life, but a fact that is just as certain as life; it has a way of catapulting itself into all our unsuspecting moments. It becomes the grim reminder at every New Year's Eve party that we are not merely watching a clock; we are watching our passing.

Death is so unwelcome a terror that we have devised a whole new glossary of terms to avoid saying the word itself. If someone has died, we would rather say that they are "gone" or "passed away" or "departed" or "entered into peace" or "crossed over to the other side." Sudden death can have some violent synonyms, like "murder," "execution," and "homicide." But we prefer to use those brutal synonyms only when necessary. Death is never desirable. Even those who commit suicide do not do it because it is filled with meaning, but because it seems less painful than living.

My purpose is not that you adopt a futile "eat, drink, and be buried" concept of life and death. However, it might well influence some to give up their unrealistic "I'll go on *ad infinitum*" philosophy of carefree existence. Death is an actuality. *Our* actuality! It is often that unwelcome intruder that leaves Schubert's greatest symphony unfinished and renders Shakespeare's Yorick meaningless. As Hamlet holds the skull of his former jester, he laments: "Alas poor Yorick!—I knew him, Horatio: A fellow of infinite jest...where be your jibes now? Your gambols? Your songs? Your flashes of merriment that were wont to set the table on a roar."[5]

Dying Unafraid

And what has the Cross to do with death? Has the Cross abolished it? No, it has redefined it. Because of the Cross, death no longer terrifies us. For after Christ's cruel death he went to be with his Father. Indeed, he died saying to a thief, "Today you will be with me in paradise" (Luke 23:43 NIV). It is the glorious triumph of his Cross that announces that to be absent from the body is to be present with the Lord (2 Cor. 5:8 KJV). Death is but the gateway to heaven. It is the porch of eternity. Now we know the truth of the matter. In dying we but trade heartbeat for glory. We go from the instant pain of our passing to the full presence of knowing the Lord face to face. "Hallelujah!" cries the spirit of that old spiritual:

> *"Sit down, brother."*
> *"Can't sit down."*
> *"Sit down, brother."*
> *"Can't sit down."*
> *"Sit down, brother."*
> *"Can't sit down.*
> *I just got to heaven*
> *And I can't sit down!"*

What definition of our life's end issues from the Cross? Our being and personality do not cease with our respiration and pulse. The Cross says pointedly that true life has no end. If we really have life, we can never know death.

Let us look at an example of death that confronted Jesus just weeks before his own death occurred. In the eleventh chapter of John's Gospel is the story of the man Lazarus who had died. Yet Jesus refused to refer to him as dead; instead he said he was asleep (John 11:11). Later, Jesus told Lazarus's sister Martha, "I am the resurrection, and the life...whosoever liveth and believeth in me shall never die" (vv. 25–26 KJV). According to Jesus, life is to be lived free of death. The Cross makes deathless living possible.

DEATH IS BUT THE GATEWAY TO HEAVEN.

The Sting

Yes, the Cross has redefined death. No longer is death to be feared. Paul phrased it this way: "Death is swallowed up in victory. O death, where is thy sting? O grave, where is thy victory?" (1 Cor. 15:54b–55 KJV).

This beautiful metaphor of death's inability to sting us can be drawn from the parallel idea that once a bee stings, it leaves its envenomed weapon in the flesh of its victim. Now it cannot fly on carrying its ugly grudge to hurt and destroy. Its power is gone. Thus did death, the ancient destroyer, meet

Jesus at the Cross and sink into God's Son the last of its venom. Now death's reign of terror is over. Like an unarmed insect, it may only buzz about us as a nuisance, but harmless in the real view. The poison is gone. The would-be killer is powerless. Death has left its venom at the Cross. The sting is gone.

In Christ, Dead or Alive

Paul could hardly be classed as a morbid person, and yet it is certainly true that he looked forward to death. This ecstasy with which he anticipated death may seem to some to be a false enthusiasm, but it was not. Paul gives his real feelings concerning life and death in Philippians:

> For, as I passionately hope, I shall have no cause to be ashamed, but shall speak so boldly that now as always the greatness of Christ will shine out clearly in my person, whether through my life or through my death. For to me life is Christ, and death gain; but what if my living on in the body may serve some good purpose? Which then am I to choose? I cannot tell. I am torn two ways: what I should like is to depart and be with Christ; that is better by far; but for your sake there is greater need for me to stay on in the body. (Phil. 1:20–24 NEB)

What the apostle says is that living in Christ is wonderful, but dying in Christ is magnificent. "To die is gain" (v. 21 NIV) is a glorious truth. One of Christianity's greatest truths is that all who believe are better off dead!

Paul had come to know this deathless living in Jesus Christ. He had discovered it to be the outcome of the Cross. Although I will discuss self-sacrifice in the next chapter, I will introduce the idea in this important context. Paul had been to the Cross; there he had come to know his Savior and had given himself in such a depth of surrender that he claimed: "I am crucified with Christ: nevertheless I live" (Gal. 2:20 KJV).

In effect, Paul was saying that he only began to live when he had crucified himself. He said that life in its abundance and eternal power had come to him only when he had put to death his own ego, ambition, and will.

It is impossible to kill what is already dead. That is why Paul counsels us to reckon ourselves "dead to sin but alive…in Christ" (Rom. 6:11 NIV). The key to not fearing death is to die ahead of time! Most people come up to the black horizon that marks the boundary of physical life, and there they plant their heels in the sand and fiercely struggle against going on over. But here and there are those who "reckon themselves dead"— their worldly desires are gone. Their treasure is not in earthly banks but is already stored in heaven (Matt. 6:20). What they own here has been given away. They have been paying it forward. Their rich inheritance has gone on ahead of them and beckons them powerfully. Because they have already died, they are unafraid.

The Life and Death Message of the Cross

God had helped Paul to pull from his own selfish existence those parts of his life that were all for himself. This amounted to a day-by-day splitting off from Paul's life the old secular and earthbound personality that was filled with delusions of grandeur and clamors for self-recognition. There was an imaginary but substantial cross on which the new Paul was nailing the old one.

The old Paul was on the cross, and the new Paul felt this was a good place for him to be. The old Paul had too long been the only Paul. The new Paul considered the desires for petty recognition—the constant haggling for the chief seats in the halls of power—to be trivial. Out of this struggle between the two Pauls came both a crucifixion and a life that would never know death. A life that was, in fact, immune to death. The Cross of Christ proclaims the profound and precious paradox that death is dead.

The life-and-death message of the Cross is a baffling paradox. Could Christ not have given us life without giving up his own? Peter Marshall once wrote:

> *The acorn cannot save itself,*
> *if it is to bud a tree.*
> *The soldier cannot save himself,*
> *if he is to save his country.*

> *Nor can the Shepherd save himself,*
> *if he would save his sheep.*[6]

Listen to the words that blazed with mockery from one of those little souls who stood before the cross: "He saved others; himself he cannot save" (Matt. 27:42a KJV). But are not those words true? If death was to die and life was to really live, Jesus *had* to die. For God, Christ's death was an "either-or" matter. God could not save his Son if he was to save us.

The Crisis of Love

The Cross is a crisis of love. In his book *The Fall*, Albert Camus tells of such a terrible quandary. Camus has his hero, Jean-Baptiste Clamence, say: "Do you know that in my little village, during a punitive operation, a German officer courteously asked an old woman to please choose which of her two sons would be shot as a hostage? Choose!—can you imagine that? That one? No, this one!"[7] The picture this suggests is that of a mother trapped between her love for her two sons. She runs between them, embracing them, trying to make a hellish choice, for she has been told that she can save one of them, but not both. Here is a soul-rending crisis of love. Such a crisis ripped into the heart of divine love at the Cross. Either we or Christ must die. For all his love, God could not save both.

This whole shattering dilemma is reminiscent of an

illustration I once heard. I suspect this story is only fiction, but its dramatic phraseology speaks of a conflict between duty and love. According to the fable, a certain engineer regulated a revolving span across a mighty river. The bridge span was so constructed that it swung on an immense steel pin to allow for the passage of tugs and barges and other river traffic. When the span was closed, it was part of the roadbed of an important and busy railway. During all his years of employment, the engineer was responsible for opening the span for river traffic and closing it for lumbering freight trains and sleek silver streamliners with their cargoes of passengers. The daily life of the bridge engineer was centered around the little control house filled with switches and levers that he knew and understood. Outside the house was a huge machine geared with immense cams and cogs whose monstrous steel teeth provided the power that swung the span back and forth over the river.

> EITHER WE OR
> CHRIST MUST DIE.
> FOR ALL HIS
> LOVE, GOD
> COULD NOT SAVE
> BOTH.

There came a day, so the parable says, that the engineer took his young son to work with him. It was an exciting day in the boy's life. With fascination he hurled question after question at his dad. He had to know about the lights and the fuse panels and the levers and the machinery all at once. But it was not until the span had swung open to allow the passage of a stream of barges that it suddenly occurred to the engineer that his son was no longer in the control house.

The father's pulse quickened as he looked down. There was nothing below except the cold, gray, concrete pier, disappearing into a river churned white by the passing traffic. Then he looked out and spied his son playing in the machinery; he was inspecting it like a government official and passing his chubby little grease-smudged hands over the gigantic armatures and shafts. The engineer was about to go out and get the boy so he could swing the span shut, when a flashing light brought to his attention the approach of a passenger train.

There was no time to retrieve his son. The span must be closed. The father's heart leaped when he realized that his son would be crushed in the gears of that machine. The ugly crisis demanded an ugly decision. Either his son would die, or a streamliner filled with hundreds of people would be doomed. With firm purpose the engineer reached for the closing lever.

As the streamliner flashed past the control house on the bridge, the engineer noticed the laughing and happy faces of the passengers through his anguished tears. In the club car they drank and ate and played cards. Elsewhere they read and relaxed and talked. Their blind detachment seared the heart of a father, who must henceforth live with the awareness that his son had died and that none of those he died to save either noticed or cared.

HUMANITY'S GREATEST SIN LIES IN ITS INDIFFERENCE TO THE HIGH COST THAT GOD PAID TO ABOLISH DEATH.

Humanity's greatest sin lies in its indifference to the high cost that God paid to abolish death. Only the death of his Son was currency enough to pay the price. At Calvary, God realized he could not save both us and his Son. With a firm purpose he reached for the switch that operated the machinery of crucifixion.

God's Son was crushed in the gears of human violence and hatred.

But from his Cross issued our own life, free forever of the necessity of dying. This marvelous and deathless living can be ours. Thanks be to the Cross! Death has died!

To have faith

is not part

of human nature,

but it is part

of human nature

that man's mind should go

against his inner instinct.

Thomas Aquinas

SUMMA THEOLOGICA

CHAPTER EIGHT

The Dying Life

THE ART OF SACRIFICING OURSELVES

Later, knowing that all was now completed, and so that the Scripture would be fulfilled, Jesus said, "I am thirsty." A jar of wine vinegar was there, so they soaked a sponge in it, put the sponge on a stalk of the hyssop plant, and lifted it to Jesus' lips. When he had received the drink, Jesus said, "It is finished." With that, he bowed his head and gave up his spirit. (John 19:28–30 NIV)

I have been crucified with Christ and I no longer live, but Christ lives in me. The life I live in the body, I live by faith in the Son of God, who loved me and gave himself for me. (Gal. 2:20 NIV)

When every second counted, the Master's time was running out. He had lived all of his life for this Friday. Now it was here. The ropes were cutting with purple savagery into his flesh. His wounded hands were numb. His head slumped forward on his chest, and sweat, mingled with blood, ran into the corners of his eyes, stinging them with spasms of blindness. Such was the end of Jesus' life.

Joseph Wittig once said, "A man's biography ought really to begin not with his birth but with his death; it can be written only from the point of view of its end, because only from there can the whole of his life in its fulfillment be seen."[1] So it is that when we tell anyone of Jesus, we must begin with his death. No one can begin to understand the life of Christ without understanding his death. "Once upon a tree…" the story begins.

"Self-sacrifice" is the most fearsome way to say "self-denial." I want to make both of these hyphenated words a part of my speech. But I must see neither word as making me grander than I really am. Both words refer to the way I use my days, how I spend the small moments with which I shall purchase the worthy years of my life. Anticipating my own dying keeps me remembering that life is inherently serious. As the wag reminds me, "I cannot get out of life alive." I must therefore let my impending death teach me how to spend the currency of my days.

ALL HUMAN LIFE IS BEING POURED OUT EITHER IN SELF-CONCERN OR IN SERVICE.

But how am I to do it? Well, the apostle Paul said that he was "being poured out as a drink offering" (Phil. 2:17a). Indeed, *all* human life is being poured out either in self-concern or in service. But it is the judgment of the Cross

146

that I should give my life as a sacrifice to the Lord, who gave his life as a sacrifice for me.

Celluloid Crosses vs. Self-Surrender

The cross seems to be an overwrought, underlived, representation of Christianity. It has degenerated into a vacuous symbol of a self-indulgent religious fraternity. Our world has literally gone "cross crazy." Crosses are manufactured in celluloid to be used as bookmarks. They are painted on automobile bumpers and displayed in plastic on dashboards. Luminous crosses are suspended on light pulls. They are worn on neck chains, embroidered on pulpit garments, welded to steeples, and built of polished wood for church altars. Cross factories manufacture crosses for a mass-production market. We have literally "crucified" the cross with overexposure!

What does God expect of me in an age which undermines Jesus' sacrifice? I must cast off the cross as kitsch if I ever regain it as the rough bloody wood of Jesus' horror. The crucified Jesus was not a figure of silver hung on polished ebony. He was not a crucifix of cold, unfeeling metal, but a human being whose blood oozed out into the chilling winds of an April morning in the third decade of the first century. It is not what the Cross *was* to Jesus, but what it *is* to me that is so crucial. I should force myself to direct my attention to the real issue of self-surrender. I should not "give myself" in an act of heroism during which I am all too conscious of the glory of my "sacrifice." Rather than phrasing my surrender as a negative, I must make it altogether in the positive mode. It is not that I herald my "giving up," but that I am absorbed in the positive passion of living for Christ. Consider the counsel of Psalm 27:4: "One thing I ask of the Lord, this is what I seek: that I may dwell in the house of the LORD all the days of my life, to gaze upon the beauty of the LORD and to seek him in his temple" (NIV).

Worthy Passions

John White counsels us: "It is time we threw spiritual pragmatism out of the window.... It is time we forgot about our spiritual performance and our spiritual needs and gave ourselves up to passion."[2]

What must I do to make the Cross my private altar? I often make spiritual submission and self-crucifixion a negative and frightening affair. As a pastor interested in the crucified life, I'm afraid I have too frequently called out to the needy, "Come to Jesus, dear sister or brother, and you will have a deep experience of being scorned, spurned, rejected, and living a miserable life. It will be just wonderful being despised, you'll see!" I ought not be so shocked that "dungeon, fire, and sword"[3] are not seen by my contemporaries as exciting enticements for coming to Christ.

Rather, the glory of self-crucifixion is not to be found in those acts in which I try to demonstrate how selfless I am. It is a state I arrive at as a result of my passion for Christ. I am so in love with him that the ardor drives me with so much vitality that I lose all sense of self in the wonder of his service. It is only when I stop to look back over my shoulder that I see a rut plowed in the sand by the cross I am bearing; in the joy of bearing that cross I had not noticed its weight. *Truly his burden is light and his yoke is easy* (Matt. 11:30).

Those who remain too conscious of their submission have experienced it in only surface ways. I once commented in *If This Be Love* that my mother raised us to own such a passion for life that we were suddenly surprised in midadolescence to realize we were poor. It was not a deception she intended to foster: It was just that her basic definition of life did not encompass "financial wealth." But the key thing I learned in midadolescence was not that we had been poor all our lives, but rather that those who considered themselves wealthy did so on the basis of such little things as bank accounts, stock certificates, and real estate holdings.

Positive passions are the only worthy passions. To grumble out my testimony, complaining about my cross, is to lose the glory of my discipleship. It was years before I learned that a certain woman in our church had given her son one of her kidneys so that he could live. When I saw his scarred abdomen as we dressed after a racquetball game, I could only gasp, "What happened to you?" He smiled and told me that his mother bore this very same set of scars; and without her scars, he said he would not have lived. I was dumbfounded, not so much by his scars or even his words, but by his smile. I noticed that she smiled a lot too. Neither of their passions would admit to any real sacrifice on either of their parts. Joy is greater than pain. What is given up is never seen as a real sacrifice between lovers. This is the way I am to feel about Jesus.

My cross, his Cross: These are the symbols of lovers, that's all. Yet to look on his Cross reminds me that cheap grace is out of the question. He gave, I give; and I have received as he received. He died and gloried in the dying that he might present me to his Father (John 17:24). I die and glory in the dying that our love might consume me with the only meaning possible in an unfeeling universe. Each day I pray, "God, sear my eyes and prevent me from weeping at the little I have given." The vast treasure of the Cross overwhelms my petty cry for heaven's charity.

> MY CROSS, HIS CROSS: THESE ARE THE SYMBOLS OF LOVERS, THAT'S ALL.

It is for this important reason that George MacLeod has written:

> I argue that the cross be raised again at the center of the marketplace as well as on the steeple of the church. I am recovering the claim that Jesus was not crucified in a cathedral between two candles, but on a cross between two thieves; on the town garbage heap; at a crossroads so cosmopolitan that they had to write his title in Hebrew and Latin and in Greek; at the kind of place where cynics talked smut and thieves cursed, and the soldiers gambled. Because that is where he died, and that is what he died about, and that is where churchmen should be and what churchmanship should be about.[4]

The Cross that ended Jesus' life is important; a cross that stands for anything else is trivial.

He Sure Looked Good on Friday

Ernest Hemingway wrote a book of short stories called *Men without Women*. One of the stories included in that book is titled "Today Is Friday." It is written in the form of a trilogy and deals with three Roman soldiers who have just crucified a Nazarene carpenter. After they crucify this carpenter, who had claimed to be the Son of God, they stop by a tavern in ancient Jerusalem on the way back to the barracks.

One of the soldiers has been unaffected by the whole incident and drinks his ale as lustily as ever. Another of the soldiers cannot forget this carpenter—he seemed like such a good fellow—but he orders himself a cup of ale and begins to drink anyway. The third soldier is slapped on the back and told to order his ale and drink it. But he cannot. His heart and mind are still back there at the scene of the Cross and on the man who was dying there.

While his raucous buddies chug-a-lug their ale, the third soldier keeps staring with a faraway look in his eyes and finally says, "He sure looked good in there today." Then there is more laughter and more table talk in the tavern. But ever and anon in the midst of ale and gaiety, the thunder-struck soldier says again, "He sure looked good in there today!"

Hemingway's story is not historical, but the reactions of these soldiers parallel some of the typical reactions of those who study the Cross. The great mass of people go through life untouched by its importance. Not many have the sense and sobriety of that serious soldier who said, "He sure looked good in there today." Hemingway correctly pictures variant opinion and reaction to the Cross.

Most of the people at the crucifixion fell into one of three categories: There were those whose reaction was discernibly negative—they might even be called "enemies of the Cross." Then there were those who simply ignored what was happening; and finally, we see those who merely watched in idle curiosity. Few had a truly positive response to the Cross and what it meant. Let us consider these three reactions to the Cross of Jesus.

Enemies of the Cross

There have always been, first of all, what we might call "the enemies of the Cross." These are the people who actually despise the Cross and its message and look on both with scorn. It seems unthinkable that the Cross, the epitome of love and sacrifice, could have enemies, but such was the case and still is. Paul realized that many hated the Cross, and it was with a broken heart that he had to write to the church at Philippi and say, "For many walk, of whom I have told you often, and now tell you even weeping, that they are the enemies of the cross of Christ" (Phil. 3:18 KJV).

There are those in every age who will throw rocks at lions as long as the beasts are caged. These people were at the Cross also. They had captured for themselves a heretic, and they were making the most of it. They circled the Cross in scorn. Their mocking, hollow words will be an indictment against them on Judgment Day.

These enemies never sought to see any purpose in the Cross; they were too busy hurling hate and slander at Jesus

(Matt. 27:39–43). One can imagine the hollow ring of their sarcasm: "Jesus, we have every confidence that you are what you say you are—the Son of God! Why don't you come down from the cross and silence our insults? You claimed to have created the world. It seems that someone whose hands had created the world could pull out three little nails and come down. Or are you so comfortable you prefer to stay?" Then someone might have spewed an insult at his kingship: "Your Majesty, King of kings! Is God your father, as you have said? Your father seems awfully unconcerned about his naked, bleeding son!"

> **THE CROSS IS INSULTED LESS BY ITS DECLARED ENEMIES THAN BY ITS PRETENDED FRIENDS.**
>
>

These enemies of the Cross said they nailed Jesus there for his blasphemous teachings. Then, when his execution was underway, they committed the same kind of sacrilege of which they had falsely accused him.

There are still many today who would sneer at the defenders of the Cross. They would say that we are wasting our devotion when we give it to a man crucified between two desperados. To many of these enemies of the Cross, Jesus was little more than a quack faith-healer and impostor.

Enemies of the Cross are always in the business of blasphemy. They forever downgrade his sacrifice, love, and divinity.

In considering the reactions to the Cross, I am reminded of the two classes of atheists. Some atheists say there is no God; others may declare there is, yet they allow him to make no functional difference in their lives. In a similar way, there are really two kinds of enemies of the Cross: those who mock the suffering Christ and those who bless his sacrificial dying but never take up a cross of their own self-surrender. The Cross is insulted less by its declared enemies than by its pretended friends.

Playing with Dice at the Foot of the Cross

The *declared* enemies of the Cross (in our country, at least) are not so common as the second category of crucifixion bystanders: those who somehow realize that the Cross is important but, because of its demands, merely *ignore* it, as perhaps even that second soldier did. These are "the undeclared enemies," like the dicers at the crucifixion who, in the moment of that great drama, were casting lots for Christ's clothing. The dicers at Calvary had a good game going, a chance to win. And winning, to the dicers, is all, so they must not be interrupted.

If it were possible to return, by way of H. G. Wells's fabled time machine, to history's greatest moment, I would like to go back to Golgotha just long enough to interrupt those who gambled at the foot of the cross. Oh, for just one opportunity to grasp the shoulders of those who played with dice and shout, "Stop this game, you fools. Don't you realize that the issue of your own souls is being determined just a few feet above your heads? The Christ of Life is dying while you play at dice!"

In a majestic moment of redemption, the gamblers whiled away their opportunities with trivialities. The dicers at Calvary were narcissists who had grown so callous in their own pursuits of bric-a-brac they could not recognize the gold they might claim.

Are we really any wiser? Do we not still ignore the Cross and focus all our attention on petty things? We have ears, yet are deaf to the utterances of the Christ impaled on our behalf. We have eyes, yet never look up to see the face of our Redeemer. Spiritually, we are playing dice at the foot of the Cross. We have our bingo societies and bowling leagues. We have bridge clubs and golf classes. We have our night-clubs, sports cars, and cocktail parties. Life for us is one grand whirl of confetti and ticker tape.

Frankly, most in our generation will not offer ourselves on the altar of Good Friday. Why? We love too much some secular Everest we think we can conquer. But in time our climb grows desperate. Our mountain defeats us! Then, we find, we are not managing life. Life is managing us. We are completely manipulated by the roster of those trivial activities we once thought important. We find ourselves tied down with a thousand Lilliputian threads, and we become the victims of our own schedules.

As we lay our self-surrender aside, we become dicers, too absorbed in the game of life to stop and ponder the issues of repentance and faith. Occasionally we seem to sense that all our worldly importance and busyness is adding up to zero, but we will not stop to discover the gift of life. We are gambling at the foot of the cross. Few of us react negatively to the Cross, as did its long-ago blasphemous enemies; rather, we do not react to it at all! If the Cross is a take-it-or-leave-it situation, we prefer simply to leave it.

The most potent threat to Christianity never comes from those who blatantly attack its truths. The greatest danger always comes from those who become ensnared in the creeping tentacles of a comfortable secularity. We never march purposefully into hell; we simply fall asleep on the slopes and slide in.

Watching Instead of Believing

Calvary reveals a third reaction to the crucifixion. The Scriptures mention a group of people who quietly observed what was happening: "And sitting down they watched him there" (Matt. 27:36 KJV). These "watchers of the cross" did not violently oppose Jesus, as did his enemies. Neither did they ignore him like the gamblers, for they were watching.

Some might even have been favorably impressed with the man on the cross, as was Hemingway's third soldier.

The crucifixion happened on a busy market day when many people were doubtless coming into the city to do their last-minute shopping for the Passover holidays. This was such an important Jewish holiday that the city was thronged with pilgrims returning to the Holy Land from every province of the Roman Empire. The Cross had likely drawn an international crowd of onlookers. They were not completely disinterested, for they had stopped to watch. Yet they were not interested in becoming involved, either.

THE LAST RAVAGES OF HUMAN EXISTENCE INVOLVE TRYING TO BE COMFORTABLE WHILE WE DIE.

These watchers saw it all. They watched the condemned man being spiked. They saw the cross as it was jolted upright in its socket. They heard the dull thud it made when it fell into its hole. They saw Jesus try in vain to position his head comfortably against the rugged vertical timber of the cross.

The last ravages of human existence involve trying to be comfortable while we die. Even those who crucify themselves in self-surrender struggle to find some way to endure the ordeal while the unyielding wood makes no place for them to cradle their heads.

The Uncomfortable Work of Self-Sacrifice

Submission is always uncomfortable work, but it is the grand virtue. St. Theresa wrote of long ago: "They deceive themselves who imagine union with God consists in ecstasies, visions, the joys of sensible devotions."[5] Submission is grand identity with Christ, who confessed that he had nowhere to lay his head (Matt. 8:20). Nowhere is the loneliness, the homelessness, the restlessness of our self-crucifixion more obvious than at the dying place.

Why is it that those who often start out as pastors or television evangelists often find their self-sacrifice gradually replaced by the good life? "All to Jesus, I Surrender" is a hymn easily replaced by "Lord, Please Give Me a Mercedes-Benz." Because the two songs are in the same musical key, it's sometimes hard to tell when we've changed either the melody or our commitment. I believe that most of the three-private-jets preachers never intended to luxuriate in their admirers' donations, but the Cross gradually grew so uncomfortable that they abandoned it in favor of a cushier life.

Rabbi Kushner commented that we can only become useful to society when we become like hunting dogs who learn to retrieve game birds in their mouths without taking a bite of them.[6] How true this is for all of us who want to live the crucified life. When God dumps his blessings upon us, it is an easy stretch to start living for the blessings rather than for God. When we finally return the prize to the Master, the prize we should have delivered whole has been half-eaten. And we say at such moments, "The laborer is worthy of his hire." Or, as Father Divine used to say, "Seek ye first the kingdom of God and all these [material] things will be added unto you" (Matt. 6:33).

KISSING LEPERS IS, OF COURSE, ACCEPTABLE ONLY TO THOSE WHO HAVE ALREADY DIED IN CHRIST.

Herein lies the greatest snare of the crucified life. People who honor God will often be admired for clothing themselves in Christ (Gal. 3:27). The trick is to live in the midst of admiration without stopping overlong before our dressing mirrors. To turn the light on Christ is to notice that a bit of it spills over on ourselves. But soon it is not focused only on Christ, but on us *and* Christ. Later it falls only on us, while Christ waits in the wings. Crucifying ourselves is therefore daily. If we forget to do it on Tuesday, and then again on Wednesday, we might never think of it again.

Kissing Lepers

Chesterton wrote of the man we now call St. Francis of Assisi. On returning from the crusades that should have but did not make him shrink in fear, he was stopped, chilled at the heart, by a leper in the road:

> Francis Bernardone saw his fear coming up the road towards him; the fear that comes from within and not without; though it stood white and horrible in the sunlight. For once in the long rush of his life his soul must have stood still. Then he sprang from his horse, knowing nothing between stillness and swiftness, and rushed on the leper and threw his arms around him. It was the beginning of a long vocation of ministry among many lepers, for whom he did many services; to this man he gave what money he could and mounted and rode on. We do not know how far he rode, or with what sense of the things around him; but it is said that when he looked back, he could see no figure on the road.[7]

Kissing lepers is, of course, acceptable only to those who have already died in Christ. When we find any contagion repugnant or beneath the dignity of what Christ asks us to do, we are still too much alive to our own self-interests.

I have never loved the scriptural Jesus more than when he faces the man who was possessed by a "legion of demons" (Mark 5:1–20). The fearsome monster, who had maimed and injured others, is restored to wholeness by the Christ whose life created life for him. The Master embraces this poor half-man, and he is whole. Hugging madmen, like kissing lepers, holds threat as being of no consequence.

Our witnessing is gloriously freed by our surrender. Chesterton sees this in the wonderful moment of Francis's conversion. The man of Assisi stood to say, "Up to this time I have called Pietro Bernardone father, but now I am the servant of God." He then piled his garments in a heap on the floor, except for his hair shirt, and walked out into the snow. Penniless and parentless, without any support or family ties, and bathed only in the mercy of his own submission, he walked off in renunciation of his once lavish life. But as he passed under the frosted trees, "he burst suddenly into song."[8]

In Zeffirelli's wonderful movie, as Frances walks away from the wealthy watchers of Assisi, he declares simply, "I am born again." The crowd pities him, but Francis is jubilant. The Cross had given him a reason to live, and the disdain that marked the faces of the onlookers was refuted by the song of freedom that set him singing in the snow.

Are We Not Guilty?

When it comes to crosses, some watch and some die to self. Those who merely watch are buried in unmarked graves; those who die to self change the world—though it is never their ambition—and are celebrated for the cross they carry constantly in their hearts.

So it was, of course, at Calvary. In watching Jesus die, a smug, self-satisfied feeling came over the crowd. They felt good about themselves, for they were not the ones who were driving the nails that day. They personally would never have flogged Jesus or ringed his brow with thorns. Such inhumane things belonged to the cruel men who had charge of the crucifixion. They only watched.

Thus they felt innocent! Were they? A similar situation, which is wholly imaginary but possible, is that of a young boy playing in the road, with an automobile bearing down on him. You know it will soon take his life, but he is not your child and it is not your fault that he is playing in the highway. You merely watch, and soon the child is bleeding and dead. Although no court in the country could possibly hold you responsible, you cannot help blaming yourself. You should have given a cry of alarm. You should have rushed out into the highway and made an attempt at rescue. You should have done something more than merely looking on. Merely looking is a grave sin when more than looking is required.

WHEN IT COMES TO CROSSES, SOME WATCH AND SOME DIE TO SELF.

Blind to His Dying

The entire idea of being crucified with Christ mandates that true Christianity can afford no mere onlookers. Those who take up their crosses have said, "The tomb I choose, wherein I reckon myself dead to sin, symbolizes my commitment. Now I am alive in Christ" (Rom. 6:11).

In the Iran-Iraq war, on the Thursday before the battle began, the Iraqi soldiers dug forty thousand graves in the lonely desert sands. They did not dig these graves for the enemies they hoped to slaughter, but for themselves. These holes signified their commitment to die for the cause. They never used them, it is true, but it is nonetheless glorious that in their minds they were more committed to death than treachery. Bonhoeffer was right. Jesus' call to "take up the cross" (Luke 9:23) was really his way of saying, "Come with me and die." Commitment to the way of the Cross is not just the pledge of martyrs, it is the password to heaven. Only the dying life is a Christian life.

This same yardstick must be applied to watchers of the Cross. When the Son of God died, none of them could be classified as innocent. There were enough onlookers, in all likelihood, to have prevented the Cross by brute strength alone. Any who stand by and do nothing to prevent injustice become guilty of the injustice themselves. Yet there is always this purely human attempt to shift the blame to someone else. So the watchers at Calvary felt a great deal better by telling themselves that the guilt for Jesus' death belonged to the execution squad.

A parallel might be drawn in our own society. A condemned man sits in an electric chair, although there is much reason to doubt he is guilty of any crime. At five minutes till midnight the electrocutioner, hooded in black, enters the room. At midnight he walks to the circuit breaker and closes the switch. There is the sizzling of electrodes. There is a fierce surging against the strap—a gurgling cry! There is the crackling sound of high voltage and heavy current. A man is dead—and perhaps he was innocent!

THE WATCHERS OF THE CROSS WERE AS GUILTY OF HIS DEATH AS THE HAMMER MAN.

The man under the black hood must rationalize his actions if he is to maintain any mental stability. So he reasons that *he* has not really taken a life; it was the judge who was responsible, for he or she handed down the sentence. The judge insists that blame rests with the jury who handed down the verdict. The jury excuses itself and points to the laws of the state, which (at least in theory) represent the will of the people. Who is responsible for the execution? Well, just about everybody, it seems.

So it was, too, at Christ's execution site. The watchers of the Cross were as guilty of his death as the hammer man. Their own failure to act in a positive way has condemned them. They have many descendants in our day. There are many who still insist that Calvary happened so long ago that they cannot possibly be implicated in the awful crime. But we who have been to the Cross understand our crime. The Cross has no innocent bystanders.

We are all guilty, if only because of our insensitivity. God lost all that he held dear on that cross. But we twentieth-century Cross-watchers are often so self-absorbed that we never feel any pity about this, much less shame. When we will not weep over the heartbreak that God experienced in the first century, we are condemned by our ugly, leaden unconcern. We must give up our stance of innocence and accept full responsibility for the Cross. We must apologize for our sins, or we forever forfeit eternity with Christ.

"God so loved the world that he gave his only Son." The cost of the project was so immense that none can claim the Cross without owning its demands. Let us exalt as our champion that nameless centurion who was gripped by the commanding majesty of Jesus Christ and confessed in choked emotion, "Surely he was the Son of God!" (Matt. 27:54 NIV). Truly, he *was* the Son of God! Hallelujah for the Cross! It is his dying! It is ours! May his crimson testament visit all the pale days of our redeemed lives with unfading color.

That glorious form, that light insufferable,

That far beaming blaze of majesty,…

He laid aside, and here with us to be,

Forsook the courts of everlasting day,

And chose with us a darksome house of clay.

John Milton

PARADISE REGAINED

CHAPTER NINE

The Piercing of Pain

THE TRIUMPH OF THE CROSS IN OUR SUFFERING

From the sixth hour until the ninth hour darkness came over all the land. About the ninth hour Jesus cried out in a loud voice, "Eloi, Eloi, lama sabachthani?"—which means, "My God, my God, why have you forsaken me?"

When some of those standing there heard this, they said, "He's calling Elijah."

Immediately one of them ran and got a sponge. He filled it with wine vinegar, put it on a stick, and offered it to Jesus to drink. The rest said, "Now leave him alone. Let's see if Elijah comes to save him." (Matt. 27:45–49 NIV)

Pain is a demon. Sometimes it stalks us. Sometimes it holds us at bay to terrorize us. Our entire nervous system can become the playing field of pain's caprice. Years ago the popular entertainer Arthur Godfrey commented on his bout with cancer by saying, "One day I never felt better in my life and then, Boom! This horrible, skulking thing visible only as a ghostly shadow on an x-ray negative…is gnawing at my vitals."[1] Pain is like that. It gathers in the dark fissures of our physiology, then leaps upon our health to reduce us to whimperings and groanings.

The Glories of the Cross

But Jesus faced the demon of pain and summoned our courage to the summit of God's purpose for it. No pain is pointless. In fact, the pain embedded in the Cross holds a glorious magnificence. On the Cross, Christ could not eliminate his pain, but he proved that hurting can become the highest work of heaven. "God is spirit" (John 4:24 NIV), but when he became a man, he voluntarily chose to take upon himself the inconvenience of a nervous system. Then came the dying time, when pain, like a reptile constrictor, wrapped its coils about the body of our Lord and ended his life. I have read the medical reports that tell how Jesus died. I understand the facts of his suffering, his suffocation, and the screaming lesions of his flesh. But my humanity forbids me understand why he elected to endure it. Other great souls may have known equal or greater pain in their passing, but Jesus volunteered for it. The glory of this condescension is that he humbled himself and became "obedient unto death, even the death of the cross" (Phil. 2:8 KJV).

Jesus is no whimpering Savior, complaining about the hurt of it all. He did cry out that he was thirsty (John 19:28), but when they offered him a narcotic, he would not drink (Mark 15:23). Why? Who can say, except that he knew there would be others in the unfolding centuries who would have to endure pain for which no narcotic would be offered. Jesus wanted to taste pain and death *in extremis* for that is how it sometimes comes.

Our God is no masochist with an odd need to suffer. He tasted death not to enjoy it but to stare it down. The glory of the Cross, as Henri Nouwen pointed out, is that Jesus was a wounded healer. To anyone who wants to know where our Messiah can be found, we must say with Nouwen,

WOUNDS BECOME A LOVING GOD.

"He is outside the city near the gates. He sits bandaged, yet he invites all those who are injured to come to him for healing." He does not heal by waving a magic wand above the hurting. Nor does he traffic in prayer cloths. His healing power derives from his own pain, from having iron spikes driven through his body. Wounds become a loving God. Only with such triumph can he offer the world his healing life.

I have seen Michelangelo's *Pietà* a few times and am always overcome by the tenderness of the mother, holding her crucified Son, whose limp body has at last let go of its fiery pain and found a sweet reprieve. But it is El Greco's *La Trinidad* that touches me most. In this great painting, the

Father is holding the crucified Son, while the dove of the Holy Spirit flutters overhead. El Greco captures Christ in the same exquisite moment of death's release from pain. He has died—but he has been received into the strong arms of his embracing Father. It is as if his wonderful Father is saying, "Come, dear Son, the pain of brutal earth is past."

But let us not characterize the pain of the Cross as merely physical. Who can say if ropes and thorns hurt more than abandonment and desertion? There were many kinds of agony confronted by our sovereign, unswerving victor. He the conqueror has become the author and finisher of our faith (Heb. 12:2 KJV). The glory of the Cross is that Jesus nullified the final effects of pain. His pain! Our pain! All pain!

I never shall forget a sister in Christ to whom I once ministered. Her cross was cancer. Her Via Dolorosa was a one-way trip through oxygen masks, rubber drainage hoses, and blinking monitors. She bore the indignity of bedpans and the cruel necessity of having some of her Christian sisters (who served round the clock as volunteer nurses) clean her body and spoon-feed her nourishment. "Every day," she wept, "I ask the Lord to deliver me from this suffering and make me just a little stronger. But no matter how hard I pray, I simply become weaker each day."

I prayed for her, of course, but I understood that the way of every cross in every life runs only in one direction. We must travel the Calvary road until the cross we are asked to carry has done its final work. Golgotha is ours as it was his. Sometimes the pain will stop only when our lives end. But in time the pain will end. In new laughter, free joy, we will then enter the presence of Christ. Our *archegos*, our first-goer will become our *finisher*—our *perfecter* in Hebrews 12:2. We will then find glory in the fact that Christ not only died for us, but that he preceded us into the unbearable world of pain.

I have come to believe that Jesus' work on the Cross has called me to serve the community of the kingdom. When pain strikes a brother or sister, I am to react instantly and with compassion. I must join my prayer and heart and tears with that of the hurting so they can feel my support. The Cross then becomes the focal point of my compassion. In the Savior's pain, I learn about the fellowship of suffering (Phil. 3:10), and I can look at my suffering comrades and say again with Paul, "We weep with those who weep" (Rom. 12:15). He is describing the caring community when he says, "If one part suffers, every part suffers with it" (1 Cor. 12:26 NIV). The glory of the Cross shines brightly when I go as a part of the community of the Cross, to shoulder someone else's pain, to help diffuse its weight.

Furthermore, I understand that Christ is there to develop within me a more in-depth humanity. Joyce Landorf writes that when she once heard someone brag, "I've never been sick a day in my life," she couldn't help but feel a bit sorry for that person. As she puts it, "Pain and illness produce a quality of aliveness within our souls like nothing else can do."[2]

There is perhaps one final glory that comes down to me from Calvary. Come with me in a momentary conjecture and see the Christ of the Resurrection. Visualize him sharing that terrific breakfast on the shore of Galilee with his disciples (John 21:1–14). They eat together in the wonderful dawn of a softly lit sunrise. As the Master breaks the bread for them, his hands reveal the stigmata of his recent ordeal. One wonders if, just for a moment, the now-alive Jesus doesn't laugh with his companions as they savor together a newer freedom than they had known before the Cross. Jesus' pain and dying are now in the past. I wonder if the resurrected Christ felt such freedom that he broke into laughter. Overcoming pain can cause us to delight in the wonderful euphoria of health. When pain is instantly gone, we are overcome by an exotic new lightness of being.

IT IS THE GIFT OF THE CROSS TO TEACH US TO KNOW SUCH JOY.

One young Jew, who was caught in the day-to-day horror of a Nazi concentration camp, took the trouble to write these words:

> *From tomorrow on*
> *I shall be sad*
> *From tomorrow on—*
> *not today.*
> *Today I will be glad,*
> *and every day*
> *No matter how bitter it may be*
> *I shall say*
> *From tomorrow on I shall be sad—*
> *not today.*[3]

Following any cross means that the joy of every moment is to be savored. It is the gift of the Cross to teach us to know such joy. What glory!

Immanuel: God with a Zip Code

Jesus' experiences with pain began, no doubt, even as he was being born in human form. The infant Jesus struggled through Mary's birth canal, sensing her own pain, until he emerged into the life that all humans know. From that first moment of "birth canal" pain, he began to move toward the Cross, where earth's greatest lessons of pain would be his—and ours.

It was from a shepherd's cave in Judea that Isaiah's word *Immanuel* first became real as a maid from Galilee cuddled her infant son to her heart. But it was not in Bethlehem that the word *Immanuel* attained its greatest meaning. The manger could not say "God with us" as convincingly as the Cross. There the God of glory became the God of gore: the God of bright pain.

What a thrilling word is *Immanuel*. God is in it with us! This is wonderful news! God steps out of his immaculate infinity into an impure humanity. When God wished to tell the world, "I am in it with you," he chose an infant's cradle. But when God wished to tell the hurting world, "I am in it with you, *regardless*," he chose the Cross. This is what St. Alphonsus Maria de Liguori meant when he wrote:

> But the Son of God, seeing man thus lost and wishing to save him from death, offered to take upon himself our human nature and to suffer death himself, condemned as a criminal on a cross. "But, my Son," we may imagine the eternal Father saying to him, "think of what a life of humiliations and sufferings Thou wilt have to lead on earth. Thou wilt have to be born in a cold stable and laid in a manger, the feeding trough of beasts. While still an infant, thou wilt have to flee into Egypt, to escape the hands of Herod. After thy return from Egypt,

thou wilt have to live and work in a shop as a lowly servant, poor and despised. And finally, worn out with sufferings, thou wilt have to give up thy life on a cross, put to shame and abandoned by everyone."

"Father," replied the Son, "all this matters not. I will gladly bear it all, if only I can save man."[4]

God Got Personal

The gods served by other world religions often preserve for themselves the comfort of uninvolvement. Like the Father of Jesus, these gods generally claim to love humanity, but they practice only a kind of long-distance love. They hurl parables, challenges, and threats from the heights where they dwell; occasionally they even cast out lightning bolts, visions, tricks, and miracles. Such gods live comfortably, kept safe by their starry distance from their suffering, needy world. Meanwhile, their poor underling subjects struggle in troubled existence, crying, praying, and weeping for their attention.

Even God, the Father of our Lord, once loved his world from a rather safe distance. He loved all his subjects, particularly those who were downtrodden. He performed a series of miracles to release the Hebrew slaves who had been stamping straw into mud for four hundred years. He split the sea, made manna, brought water from a fissure in a wall of rock, and delivered his laws to Moses. In the ages preceding

Christ, God wanted people to know him, but he disclosed himself only in impersonal ways: through burning bushes, budding almond rods, and the like.

But God got personal at Bethlehem. He left that far-off, never-never land of heaven and came to a planet that must have seemed a pigsty by comparison. Then, for thirty-three years, men had a positive, tangible proof that "God was in it with us." There he was—Creator of the cosmos—jostled among camel drivers, questioned by scholars. The great God of an immaculate, untouchable heaven learned some very earthy traits: laughing, weeping, hurting, dying.

Once upon a tree, Jesus the Son died, and Immanuel became the involved God! In this involvement, he learned my heartache and pain by experience. At the Cross, God taught me something his aloofness had obscured: I neither live nor die alone. In Christ I see how distant and useless are all other gods. Flaunting their "foreverness" in the face of my grieving, they know nothing of my pain. How wonderful is my God! He learned about my suffering by suffering himself. And he came to understand my death by dying.

MY HEALING LIES IN HIS STRIPES, MY HEALTH IN HIS WOUNDS.

Shusaku Endo, that noble Japanese Christian, believed that the reason Jesus hadn't made much of an impact on the

Japanese people was that they didn't understand the crucified Christ, the Jesus who rendered himself powerless for their salvation. They understood the beauty and majesty of Jesus' life, but had never grasped the glory of his dying. I fear that this sacrificial Christ is the Christ we, too, tend to avoid, for just a glimpse of the dying Savior places great demands on us. God spoke through Isaiah to describe the wonder of his Suffering Son:

> He hath no form nor comeliness; and when we shall see him, there is no beauty that we should desire him. He is despised and rejected of men; a man of sorrows, and acquainted with grief: and we hid as it were our faces from him; he was despised, and we esteemed him not. Surely he hath borne our griefs, and carried our sorrows: yet we did esteem him stricken, smitten of God, and afflicted. But he was wounded for our transgressions, he was bruised for our iniquities: the chastisement of our peace was upon him; and with his stripes we are healed. (Isa. 53:2b–5 KJV)

Here I can see the far pavilions of health—health eternal, in a land where God forbids my tears and drives my pain into the abyss. So I must dance at last beneath the Cross. Jesus tasted iron—driven through his hands and feet. But mine are whole. *"De profundis clamavi,"* said Jerome's

psalmist (Ps. 129:1 in the VULGATE, Ps. 130:1 in the KJV)—
"Out of the depths I call." The pain of Christ has erased all
pain forever. My healing lies in his stripes, my health in his
wounds. Because he hurts, my pain is over. I understand
Jesus' pain. I know what he meant when he told me to take
up my cross daily (Luke 9:23). None of us knows the exact
price of his dying. Who can measure it? But because of it, I
must not expect my life to be completely free of crucifixion—
whether physical, social, or mental. To be involved with his
Cross is to take up my own. In time I, too, must be involved
with pain, but only for a while. My cross, like his, is temporary.
In time I, too, will step from Golgotha to the grand gates.
There my scars, like his, will be the glistening reminders of
my triumph.

The Cross of Mercy Is the Tree of Justice

Carlyle once protested that Emerson lived a sheltered
and peaceable life and never let anything unpleasant into
his scheme for living. According to Carlyle, Emerson
wanted no worrisome pebbles making ripples in this placid
pool of existence. Emerson seemed to Carlyle to be an unrealistic person so uninvolved with trouble that he could not
be taken seriously when he gave advice to the troubled. He
was like a complacent lifeguard who keeps himself dry while
throwing friendly chitchat to drowning swimmers battling
for life itself in their insurgent seas of troubles.

Had it not been for the Cross, this very accusation might have been laid at the feet of the God of Judaism.

The pain of Calvary is God-sized. God faced a dilemma in A.D. 27— a conflict between mercy and justice. God also realized that I was trapped in my sin and could not free myself of it. Sin, that clinging grit of Eden, is like a sticky piece of candy that a child pulls from the right hand only to find it stuck to the left. It was not enough for God to *know* my predicament. He must *feel* it. To feel it, he must have flesh that could feel the bite of my pain and the erosion of my contagions—flesh that, like mine, could be crucified. So God became flesh—corpuscle and neuron—that he might understand my pain firsthand. Only by experiencing death could he really offer me life.

A more ordinary illustration may convey the urgency of our need and the nature of God's response. Suppose a father has taken his family on a picnic at the seaside. It is the most fun they have had together in a good while. The charcoal is gleaming crimson in the brazier. The steaks lie crowded together on aluminum foil. The family can hardly wait until this out-of-doors banquet is finally underway.

Suddenly the father looks around and sees that a child is missing. His first impulse is to look toward the sea. Instinctively, he hurries toward the rushing waters. Ordinarily, he loves the sea's beauty, but now he is filled with dread by the very thought of its power. As he quickens his pace, he remembers telling the child to stay close by, but he blames himself for giving all his attention to secondary concerns. He rushes to the shoreline, where he searches for footprints in the sand. Then he sees his child, already swept too far out by the tide to be talked back to safety. If that dearest part of the father is to be rescued, he must dive into the cruel waves himself.

IF I AM TO BE DELIVERED, GOD MUST THROW ASIDE HIS DIGNITY AND DIVE INTO THE UNPREDICTABLE SURF OF SIN AND HUMAN SUFFERING.

Why is my praise of Christ so jubilant? It is I who am in the distant sea. I am the disobedient child lost at too great a distance from heaven's safety. If I am to be saved, God must get wet. Praise be to God's dilemma! He could no longer merely call to me from the safety of eternity's shoreline. My predicament is too serious for that. If I am to be delivered, God must throw aside his dignity and dive into the unpredictable surf of sin and human suffering. The Cross is the result of God's wonderful willingness to get involved. As Helmut Thielicke wrote:

Jesus Christ did not remain at base headquarters in heaven, receiving reports of the world's suffering from below and shouting a few encouraging words to us from a safe distance. No, he left the headquarters and came down to us in the frontline trenches, right down to where we live and worry about what the Bolsheviks may do, where we contend with our anxieties and the feeling of emptiness and futility, where we sin and suffer guilt, and where we must finally die. There is nothing that he did not endure with us. He understands everything.[5]

Immanuel: God in the Trenches

In another of his books, Dr. Thielicke says that it is impossible to learn war in a theater. It occurred to me, after reading this statement, that this is the only kind of war I have ever known. Having been born at a particular blessed time that made me too young to be involved in one war and too old for the next, I have never served my country in uniform. The only war I have ever known I have seen in theaters or on television. I have only vicariously experienced the incandescence of bursting shells. I have only heard the ear-shattering thunder of stereophonic explosives. No one would say that I know what war is like. The closest I have ever come to knowing war was during my pastoral visits to veterans' hospitals. There I beheld yesterday's soldiers as today's amputees. For me there was never any war, yet for them the war rages always. The old battlefields live. The pain continues. They once met the Pale Horse of Death in distant foxholes. They now know the daily judgment that rides with this Cossack of hell!

But the Cross is there to say that God was no mere spectator in our war against emptiness and death. In Christ, God did not merely observe our coming death. He suffered it ahead of time to prove to us that death is nothing more than the "lights out" call before the luminaries of eternity burst into unfading incandescence. Lights out! Lights on! He is with us!

By the time Jesus broke the loaves of Maundy Thursday, he was so much "in it" with us that he served the single longing of his Father. In the great galactic heart of God, human pain was already on the run. Jesus could have safely left Jerusalem at Passover time. He could have quietly slipped out of the garden before his arrest. He knew all that would happen. For him there were no surprises in Gethsemane; he had plenty of time to escape. Even after he was taken into custody, he was in no real danger. By his own admission, he was the Supreme Commander of an immense infantry of angels who would have delivered him from the cross at a mere word (Matt. 26:53).

But he was committed to dying.

I doubt that Jesus *wanted* to die; but I do believe that from the very beginning of his earthly ministry, he understood its necessity. That necessity was what led him to say, "Except a corn of wheat fall into the ground and die, it abideth alone: but if it die, it bringeth forth much fruit" (John 12:24 KJV). This necessity also entailed the unavoidable pain.

Nevertheless, I cannot see Jesus as a masochistic martyr. He was only thirty-three, at which age no healthy man would wish himself dead, particularly not Jesus! One sees him as a robust man totally in love with life. He loved to scoop his arms full of children to learn from them their simple wisdom. He was the sort of man who never took for granted the splendor of a Galilean sunset as it ignited the broad skies with celestial fire and then settled on the misty, beige waters of Tiberias. This man Jesus cherished the harmony in everything his Father touched, and he knew of nothing his Father had not touched.

> BY THE TIME JESUS BROKE THE LOAVES OF MAUNDY THURSDAY, HE WAS SO MUCH "IN IT" WITH US THAT HE SERVED THE SINGLE LONGING OF HIS FATHER.

Three decades of life had not made Jesus weary of life or left him suicidal and ready to die. There were so many sermons he had not yet preached. So much misery and hunger he had not yet addressed. He longed for a thousand more quiet chats with his friends in Bethany. He loved good food and great conversation. He enjoyed the out-of-doors living he shared with his twelve friends. But his role in the pageant of life was drawing to a close. His Cross was falling like the final curtain in the grand theater of life.

There at his Cross lay the greater issue—our salvation. This took the reins of purpose and placed all destiny in the unscarred hands of God. He put away those wonderful things he so loved. Then surveying the meaninglessness of human dying he asked courageously, "Father, what wilt thou?" God answered the question with a squadron of soldiers dispatched for his arrest.

In the few hours that followed, God spoke with pointed syllables the word *Immanuel*. But keep this straight: *Immanuel* does not mean "God *was* with us." It means "God *is* with us." What a depth of meaning Isaiah's grand word took upon itself! "God is with us" when justice is a farce. "God is with us" when well-meaning friends desert us. "God is with us" when our purity and integrity are challenged by unholy circumstances. "God is with us" when we become the object of expensive human sport. "God is with us" when we probe in vain for acceptable answers to cruel questions. Immanuel is here today!

Death Songs and Better Anthems

William Blake said on his deathbed, "My death songs are not mine."[6] I don't know all he meant by this, but I can guess his best lesson. Christ was with William Blake in his pain. For Blake the Cross was the symbol of God's continuing presence—even in his dying.

I had a boyhood chum who never in the early years of our friendship was open to the issue of his own surrender to Christ. After adolescence, we were separated for forty years. At last the company he worked for moved him to the city where I had become a pastor. Our friendship was reestablished. At our first meeting he informed me he was carrying a terrible judgment; he was soon to die of cancer.

In the months that he had left to live, my friend embraced Christ as his Savior. Pain was his constant companion, but so was Christ. Somehow the glory of the Christian faith became our absorbing interest. We spoke in his final weeks almost entirely of Christ; we rejoiced in the truth that in heaven there would be no death, no crying, no pain (Rev. 21:4). It was as if the ever-present Christ, by promise of a painless eternity, was healing my friend of pain through the glorious power of the surrendered moment.

The surrendered moment! Pain will not produce such surrender, but it is forced to admit it is only temporary. It appears to end in death, but in reality it ends in life. As God had come so long ago to be the Incarnate Christ, my beloved friend also became an incarnation of Christ, teaching all he met the "Immanuel victory" over death and dying.

Jesus is our contemporary Savior, our right-now Immanuel. He walks our malls, rides our freeways, flies our airlines—with *us*. He will never leave us or forsake us (Heb. 13:5). He is ours, now and forever. Immanuel! Yesterday! Today! Tomorrow!

> *How shall we ever cease to sing*
> *The ageless Christ of suffering*
> *Who took the steel as hammers fell*
> *To teach us on the brink of Hell*
> *To speak the word Immanuel.*[7]

Because upon
the first glad Easter day,
The stone that sealed
his tomb
was rolled away,
So through the
deepening shadows
of death's night,
Men see an open door...
beyond it, light!

Ida Norton Munson
EASTER LIGHT

CHAPTER TEN

The Triumph of Transcendence

LIVING HERE, LIVING SOMEWHERE ELSE, BUT EVER LIVING

He said to them, "It is not for you to know the times or dates the Father has set by his own authority. But you will receive power when the Holy Spirit comes on you; and you will be my witnesses...to the ends of the earth."

After he said this, he was taken up before their very eyes, and a cloud hid him from their sight.

They were looking intently up into the sky as he was going, when suddenly two men dressed in white stood beside them. "Men of Galilee," they said, "why do you stand here looking into the sky? This same Jesus, who has been taken from you into heaven, will come back in the same way you have seen him go into heaven." (Acts 1:7–11 NIV)

Come! Bow your head before the whispered thunder of the Savior's final words. Do his last words seem too ordinary to heal your brokenness? Are they too simple to suture all the world's wounds? Are they too confounded, unfounded, dumbfounded? Could our dying Christ have said something more dramatic?

It is incorrect to say that the story was over when the whispers of Christ's breath faded into stillness beneath the mocking letters I.N.R.I.: *Jesus of Nazareth, the King of the Jews.* If his splendid life ends there, the rest of his story is nothing

WE MUST GLORY IN THIS RICH MYSTERY THAT CREATES OUR HOPE. ERASE THIS MYSTERY, AND HOPE IS STRICKEN FROM THE DICTIONARY.

more than a powerless piece of human fiction. But the drama rolls. The story is not over. Two of his influential friends, Nicodemus and Joseph of Arimathea, come to unfasten the Master from the wood, wrap him in a shroud, and entomb him. It is touching to realize that two of his wealthy friends cared this much for him. As touching as it is, however, one still must ask, "Is there any real meaning in this tragic event?" Either Calvary must end with something more significant than the sentimental burial of a kindly carpenter or we who believe must be willing to replace it with something more redeeming.

It is not Jesus' death and his over-hasty burial that offers us real meaning. The real glory of Christianity is its Easter splendor. The Cross symbolizes only his dying, but the Resurrection is God's offering of life.

The Cross—as sacrificial as it is—can never speak to us of the greatest truth of our faith: *transcendence.* Let us not be afraid of this word. It simply means that the most valuable parts of all we believe cannot be objectified or proven "scientifically." Jesus is alive. Notice I did not say *was* alive but *is* alive. Yes, Jesus is alive! *You mean alive, now? Not possible!* Ask any coroner. Yet it is true. He lives! How shall we glory in what we can never understand? Yet we must glory in this rich mystery that creates our hope. Erase this mystery, and hope is stricken from the dictionary.

Transcendent truths are like that. They are hard to believe because they exceed the limits of human experience and punch holes in the inflated categories of possibility. It is, we must admit, a monstrous mystery. It was doubted by the apostles themselves until they first encountered their risen Lord (Luke 24:11). While the disciples admitted that dead men as a whole don't live again, they had to face this fact: Their Master did! And their lives were radically changed by this overwhelming reality. They had no choice but to go out and preach the Resurrection. The good news didn't go over too well with some of the people they tried to convince. They told the Sanhedrin (Acts 4:10) their impossible tale, but these priests and elders didn't believe. They even told the Sanhedrin a second time (Acts 5:30–32), but they still refused to believe. When Stephen told them a third time, they became so enraged they stoned him to death (Acts 7). Paul finally and reluctantly accepted the mystery, but only after he was knocked off his beast on the way to Damascus (Acts 9:1–19). Paul got paid back for his reluctance to believe, for only a few believed him when he preached the Resurrection in Athens (Acts 17:16–34). In Caesarea, King Agrippa was not convinced. When Festus, governor of Judea, heard Paul's testimony, he stood and shouted, "You are out of your mind, Paul! Your great learning is driving you insane" (Acts 26:24 NIV).

Calvary may be viewed as a historical fact. But the Resurrection is more than mere history—it is transcendent truth. Yet this kind of truth is the greatest truth and the grand imperative that creates the Christian faith. The Greek word *anastasis* means "to stand again." And so he did! And when our Savior stood that first Easter, his new life was the great transcendent truth of the Resurrection. Christianity set this truth central and above its every other claim—in fact it cannot survive without this truth. In his poem "Seven Stanzas at Easter," John Updike wrote:

> *Make no mistake: if He arose at all*
> *it was as His body;*
> *if the cells' dissolution did not reverse, the molecules*
> *reknit, the amino acids rekindle,*
> *the Church will fall.*
> *Let us not mock God with metaphor,*
> *Analogy, sidestepping transcendence;*
> *making of the event a parable, a sign painted in the*

faded credulity of earlier ages:
let us walk through the door.
Let us not seek to make it less monstrous,
for our own convenience, our own sense of beauty,
lest, awakened in one unthinkable hour, we are
embarrassed by the miracle,
and crushed by remonstrance.[1]

The Christ of the Present Moment

The Christian church at the beginning of the twenty-first century is in great doctrinal danger. It is not only "side-stepping" transcendence; it is abandoning it altogether. What has brought about this deplorable state? Who can say? Perhaps we have grown too matter-of-fact and scientific about our bodies. I see nothing unspiritual about donating our bodies to science and our organs to help others live. Living wills are a smart way to be judicious in the stewardship of our physiology. But is it possible that in frankly discussing such an economical use of our bodies we have begun to assume that we are only gristle and bone—a tissue-bank of interchangeable vessels and organs?

The more we live in our stainless-steel, computerized technocracy, the less we hear preachers talking about heaven, hell, or eternity. Although Jesus is fervently preached by most contemporary preachers, he is mostly a Jesus of the present moment. The Jesus of the evangelical world is rapidly in danger of becoming the Christ who handles current stress or makes us as popular as politicians for our show-biz, here-and-now congregations. In past generations churches were criticized for being too absorbed in the "pie in the sky by and by," but now we are hearing less and less of sky-pie, and more and more of how Jesus is little more than a grand dessert for the present moment.

The church's ultimate question once was *ultimate!* It dealt with eternity. Our hymns were about "The Sweet By and By," "Beulah Land," and "Zion" to which "we were marching." And Zion was a land as real as Chicago in the rural church in which I found Christ. Today Chicago is the more real. We don't use the word *saved* in any ultimate sense. Hell, once a never-ending category, is now only bad conditioning or ghetto sociology. Psychologists have brought a new counsel to God's people, and while their counsel is helpful in the all-important world of relationships, it makes little sense of the importance of the coming world.

The depravity of our sermons is that they have forgotten to mention that there is a new world on the way. We speak of Jesus only in terms of his power over our current misery. We almost never mention that he is also the Christ of the New Jerusalem or that, one day in the future, Christ will descend from God out of heaven.

Recently I preached a sermon to a large gathering of

evangelicals in which I referred to hell, the destiny of those who die outside of Christ. While the reference was made in passing, I was told afterward that the reference "marred" my presentation. We have arrived at a here-and-now theology, it seems, in which every transcendent category is lost.

THE DEPRAVITY OF OUR SERMONS IS THAT THEY HAVE FORGOTTEN TO MENTION THAT THERE IS A NEW WORLD ON THE WAY.

Chip Conyers, a friend of mine, told me about being shown through a pre-Revolutionary cemetery in Charleston, South Carolina. The guide was pointing out the various tombstones and commenting on those who were buried there. The history buffs in the group were fascinated by the tombstones of these founders of the American dream. Noticing that so many of the two- and three-hundred-year-old stones had weather-eroded inscriptions like "Entered Immortality, July 3, 1756" or "Gone to God, May 3, 1734," the guide said, "You will observe that many of the remarks are about the afterlife, but we all know how we feel about this!" Then the guide winked at the battery of tourists who were furiously scratching his remarks onto their note sheets. My friend said it was the wink that unnerved him so. For that wink signified the tragic loss of transcendent truth in our day.

Calvary: User-*Un*friendly

Jesus' victory over death is inseparable from his teachings about eternity. There is little use in preaching that Jesus
came back from the dead if there was no heaven for him to
inherit. He taught us that there are afterlife categories:
heaven and hell. These destinies are as true and transcendent as his own emergence from the tomb. Let us not make
of the risen Christ a homeless Messiah who, having returned
from the dead, is only a vagrant without a heaven to claim.

In a sense, the church-growth movement has con-
tributed to this loss of transcendence. It has majored on the
gospel that twenty-first-century people *want* to hear rather
than on the one they *need* to hear. Many of the megachurch
pastors speak with pride of building multi-thousand-member
churches with a gospel that is "user-friendly." To start these
churches, they often, of their own admission, asked their
community constituency what kind of church and sermons
it would take to get them to attend church. Once the community had dictated what the church must be to get their
support, the church determined to become all its con-
stituents demanded.

While it is difficult to imagine Jeremiah or Jesus starting a church in this way, the populist definition in many
cases has determined the teachings of the megachurch.

When we allow the world to define the church, we may
be sure that many of the transcendent categories of faith

will be missing. Why? Because they seem unessential in the here-and-now technocracy. Most community residents are not enthusiastic about sermons on heaven, hell, and the crucified life. They prefer something that gently massages their narcissism with "how-to" and "fix-it" messages. Thus, transcendence takes a backseat to sermons on stress, relationships, and leisure-entertainment homilies. As the transcendent is increasingly ignored, the heavenless, hell-less, resurrectionless gospel is glitzed with humor and bright lights—and the gospel message sent to deliver us from meaninglessness loses its soul.

The Last Things Jesus Talked About

In the Cross itself are hidden four of Christ's "last words," which testify to his transcendence and to the reality of eternity. If we look at them together, we shall see that the Cross and the Resurrection are one. For in God every truth is transcendent. It is not as though the Cross is the prisoner of time and her sister, the Resurrection, is liberated from history. No, they are both part of God's great transcendent Incarnation. The Jesus who died was not of this earth (John 6:38; 18:36). Yet throughout his life on earth, he preached the importance of things eternal.

"My God, why...?" (Matt. 27:46) is a cry from the cross reminding us that he dies talking to his Father. This bit of conversation, along with his prayers asking God to forgive his executioners (Luke 23:34), proves that Jesus' whole life was an unending conversation with the transcendent realm beyond the here and now. This unbroken dialogue with his Father should be enough to establish the reality of eternity.

But there are other cross-cries: "Father, into thy hands I commend my Spirit" (Luke 23:46) and "It is finished" (John 19:30) are signals from the cross that the whole transcendent plan of God is completed. Here it must be that God stamps an A on the celestial report card. Jesus is not speaking of his own death, saying "I am finished." He is saying that the Incarnation with its magnificent objectives is done. We are saved; heaven—transcendent heaven—is peopled with all who will believe.

But the cross-cry that most clearly addresses the transcendent world is this: "Today you will be with me in paradise" (Luke 23:43 NIV). Here from the cross we see the juncture of the present and the eternal. We are taught the utter truth of two who are dying. Redeemer and renegade, through suffocation and blood, look past their pain. And where their languid eyes focus, we can see the dim outlines of the celestial city. Stephen at his death saw it, too. He looked past the gates of paradise to the very throne room and said in effect, "Kill me if you must, for my death will but be my promotion. For I see heaven open and the Son of Man standing on the right hand of God" (Acts 7:56).

From the cross the testimony continues to spill forth.

There is a living Christ, and there is a heaven; and the best truths are transcendent. John cried in the Apocalypse, "I was in the Spirit on the Lord's Day…and I saw among the lampstands someone like a Son of man…and his voice was like the sound of rushing waters" (Rev. 1:10, 13, 15). Paul spoke of being caught up to the third heaven (2 Cor. 12:2), and Isaiah said, "I saw the Lord seated on a throne, high and exalted" (Isa. 6:1 KJV).

Jesus: Dynamic Despair

What then are we to make of this transcendence? The Cross must be our teacher. How will the Cross do its work? Well, to begin with, we must not tell the story of Christ as the tale of a deceived but well-meaning martyr. To see clearly the outcome of the Cross, we first allow the purple shadows of Good Friday to steal hope, purpose, and meaning from everything that Jesus ever claimed. Then we must see the gray dawn of the middle day, when the Son of God, reduced to a human corpse, lay silent in the grave. Here was despair that could find no resolution. To every eye it appeared that he was dead—forever dead! Wrapped in silent parables and soundless songs, he who claimed to be "the life" was dead. The mists of that middle day blurred eyes with grief and gripped the hearts of believers with the painful consciousness that they had given him their allegiance in vain. So the weary weekend plodded between midnights, when even the daylight was dark. And at just that place where the long, long, second day faded into the third, God wrote his victorious epilogue to Friday's defeat.

The Cross was God's finest effort to demonstrate his love, but we would never have stopped to consider it without the Resurrection. And, without the majesty and sacrifice of the Cross, we would have forgotten the Resurrection in a fortnight. Both are imperative to our faith.

The weird hypothesis that Matthew Arnold presented in *Obermann Once More* is untrue:

> *Now he is dead! Far hence he lies*
> *In the lorn Syrian town,*
> *And on his grave with shining eyes,*
> *The Syrian stars look down.*

To be sure, this is where the Cross leaves Jesus—alone and dead in a Middle East tomb. Were the Cross the end of it all, someone might someday discover Jesus' grave covered by the debris of time. Since that first Easter, however, it has been and will be forever impossible to find a headstone marked "Jesus of Nazareth" with the date of his decease chiseled out in Roman numerals. He is alive! God has raised him from the dead! Easter has become the pier on which personal salvation rests. So imperative is the Resurrection truth for mankind that none can know salvation without believing it. Paul wrote: "That if thou shalt confess with thy mouth the Lord

Jesus, and shalt believe in thine heart that God hath raised him from the dead, thou shalt be saved" (Rom. 10:9 KJV).

Alive Again!

As previously mentioned, when Paul made his defense before Agrippa and Festus, he spoke of how he had come to believe in Christ. His testimony was well received until he made mention of the Resurrection, then he was accused of madness. When Paul spoke on Mars Hill, the logicians balked at his speaking of the Resurrection. Where the Cross gives way to the crown, Christianity becomes hard for many to believe. Logicians always object to a concept that defies "sound reasoning," as the Resurrection surely does. But Christians defend their belief in the Resurrection of Christ as vigorously as they defend the Cross.

If the Resurrection seems hard for us, who have the New Testament witness as a backdrop, we can see how hard it must have been for the core of Christ's disciples, who were confronted by it without the advantage of our historical perspective.

Imagine the women at the tomb as they discover that the dead Jesus is really alive. Babbling excitedly, they rush to report the news to the apostles. Understandably, the apostles are dumbfounded by the incoherent chatter of these women and are skeptical of their report.

Then Jesus, every whit alive, walks in on them. They are

gripped by the terror that springs from the realm of ghosts and ghouls and things that go bump in the night. Two or three of them pinch themselves to be sure they are awake. Others try to talk themselves out of what their eyes clearly tell them is there. All of them blink as though the rapid shutting of their eyelids will erase the specter. Suddenly, like a radiant burst of glory, the same truth dawns on them that had come earlier to those excited women. It is true! Jesus is alive!

"And if Christ be not risen, then is our preaching vain, and your faith is also vain" (1 Cor. 15:14 KJV). The *sine qua non* of our faith is the Resurrection. This is the outstanding, unique factor of Christianity. We do not embrace the Christian religion because there was a Cross, but because the outcome of the Cross was the Resurrection. If Christ is still dead, what real improvement is Christianity over a score of other lofty philosophies? Either Christ has risen from the grave or we are fools for believing so. Either Christ is alive or the Cross was a black hour, for it was the end of a brilliant little starburst of ethics and positivism. Either the Resurrection happened or the Cross must issue this solemn pronouncement: "Alas, he was only a man, and we have stolen his life and breath. Too

> IF CHRIST IS STILL DEAD, WHAT REAL IMPROVEMENT IS CHRISTIANITY OVER A SCORE OF OTHER LOFTY PHILOSOPHIES?

bad! Bury your Bibles, we have no Father. God has no Son. We are all orphans."

Thomas and the Tomb

In its earliest discovery by the women, the Resurrection is a joyful madness. According to John's account, after seeing him alive, they ran to bring the report to John and Simon Peter, who rushed to the empty tomb and "believed" when they saw the discarded burial cloths. Soon afterward, Jesus appeared to his disciples, though Thomas was not with them at the time.

One can imagine Simon Peter telling Thomas about it later: "Thomas, we have seen the Lord! He's alive!" But Thomas is skeptical about such an impossibility. He sticks his tongue in his cheek and shakes his head "yes" in such a way that you can tell he means "not a chance of it." Then Thomas says, "Sure, Peter—sure, you did! Get real, man!" Then he adds explosively, "Who in the world do you think you're trying to outwit? Peter, we all know he died. Did he not try in vain to cradle his head against the vertical beam of the cross? Did he not struggle for breath till his faithful head slumped forward on his lifeless breast? Did not the man with the spear make sure he was dead? It was gruesome, but I saw it all. He's dead, Peter!"

Then perhaps Thomas would have leveled the same charge of insanity against the report of the apostles that they had earlier laid at the feet of the women. "My dear friends," Thomas might have said, "you have not seen Jesus. At least, you have not seen him alive. You have been in the sun too long without your turbans. You saw a man in a seamless robe whose stature was the same, perhaps. You saw some bulk in the dark and mistook it for Jesus. Maybe you dreamed he was alive. And Peter, you saw him because you loved him so much that you wanted to see him.

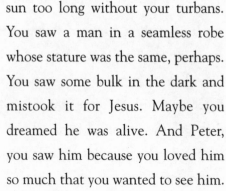

MEN WILL SOMETIMES TELL LIES, BUT THEY WILL NOT DIE FOR THOSE LIES.

I loved him, too, but get hold of yourself. None of us will ever see him again. He's dead! Dead! *Dead!*"

Then come more of those "silent" days when Jesus does not show himself to his apostles. Finally, when Thomas is present with the others, the matchless Master of Life breaks in on the reverie of the group. Thomas, his doubts now erased, falls down in submission to the Christ of Kept Promises and says in a voice choked with emotion, "My Lord and my God!" (John 20:28 NIV).

Resurrection: A Current Verb with No Past Tense

It was not easy for the disciples to accept the Resurrection; they were too close to it. It was impossible for them to stand back from a distance of twenty centuries and view it objectively as we do. But accept it they did! In truth, nearly all of them were later martyred, rather than say it did not happen. Men will sometimes tell lies, but they will not die for those lies. Each of these men died still clinging to the "unbelievable" transcendent truth that Jesus had risen from the dead. As Peter Marshall once said, the Resurrection is "historically" true:

> The resurrection of Christ was regarded by the disciples as something which is as indisputable historically as the death of President Wilson. It did not occur to them, as they spoke or as they wrote, to argue about it, any more than it would occur to a senator making a speech to say: "Since the death of President Wilson, *that is to say if he is really dead.*"[2]

As surely as Pontius Pilate was a real historical figure, so was Jesus of Nazareth. As surely as the Cross really happened, so did the Resurrection become its joyous outcome. In contrasting the importance of the Cross and the Resurrection, we need to remind ourselves that Christ was dead for only three days, but he has now been alive for two thousand years. His return from the grave is the all-important victory that has kept Christianity out of the graveyard of other lofty philosophies and religions. So we must forget the "Messiah of the media" who uses so much movie film to die and so little to rise again. The Resurrection is too important to be shelved as an "incidental" area of Jesus' existence and teaching. We must cease this business of talking as though his return to life was only momentary then over. The Resurrection is not in the past tense. It is continuous, right down to the present. His life extends across all time from the Caesars until now. His Resurrection is the recurrent theme in the symphony of the centuries; the golden thread woven throughout the fabric of time.

The Resurrection meant triumph to the disillusioned apostles who had given Christ their livelihood, allegiance, and devotion. It is also *our* only shot at hope and meaning. His life is our life, too. We have no life if he does not live.

Sky-Pie, Anyone?

The greatest human truth is transcendent. He is alive. We are alive. We will allow no one to wink at us and tell us his Resurrection is "sky-pie." The earth quaked, the rocks split, and Jesus walked out of the tomb. His very footfalls made hell tremble and shook the foundations of history. So, when the unborn sun of any Easter morning shoots its shafts of promise through the East, let us remember that God is ever there to restore our crushed hopes and awaken our temporary lives to get dressed for eternity. How marvelously God knows how to spell *triumph*.

Once upon a tree the Son of God was crucified, but death could not hold him.

Job long ago sought the answer to one plaguing question:

"If a man die, shall he live again?" We now have the answer! Job shall live again! We will share in his answer. It makes no matter how we die, for even the excruciating and torturous death of the Cross was illusory and not binding. Death is not a threat to genuine life. It is but a paper tiger no longer free to terrorize. We know the truth about crosses. They are hazardous to health. But never mind! Death is but a temporary inconvenience. *Life* is the only word emblazoned on the gates of glory. The Resurrection is a crown of triumph on the wounded head of tragedy. The despair of Good Friday has been superseded. Easter dawns eternal!

Is it not odd that the world's most glaring light should issue from a tomb?

> *The grave of Christ—resplendent blight—*
> *Where Easter came to spend the night*
> *Has left us squinting at the sight*
> *To shade our eyes against such light*
> *And cry he is alive and so are we!*
> *Hallelujah!*[3]

Notes

CHAPTER TWO

1. Bruce Cockburn, cited in Gail & Jill Perry, eds., *A Rumor of Angels* (New York: Ballantine Books, 1989), 111.

2. Dylan Thomas, "Do Not Go Gentle into That Good Night" (1952).

3. Francis Thompson, "The Hound of Heaven" (1893).

4. Priscilla J. Owens, "Jesus Saves!" *The Hymnal for Worship and Celebration* (Waco, Tex.: Word Music, 1986), #306.

5. Fanny J. Crosby, "Near the Cross," *The Hymnal for Worship and Celebration* (Waco, Tex.: Word Music, 1986), #385.

CHAPTER THREE

1. John Bowring, "In the Cross of Christ I Glory," *Baptist Hymnal* (Nashville: Convention Press, 1975), #70.

2. Thomas Moore, "Come, Ye Disconsolate," *The Hymnal for Worship and Celebration* (Waco, Tex.: Word Music, 1986), #416.

3. Thomas Dooley, *The Night They Burned the Mountain* (as condensed in *Reader's Digest 40th Anniversary Treasury*, The Reader's Digest Association, 1961), 341–342.

4. Thomas à Kempis, *The Imitation of Christ*, trans. Abbot Justin McCann (New York: New American Library, 1959), 147.

CHAPTER FOUR

1. Avis B. Christianson, "Blessed Redeemer," *Baptist Hymnal* (Nashville: Convention Press, 1975), #109.

2. Charles Malik, "Trust Your Instincts, Mrs. Jones!" *Guideposts* 16 (May 1961), 5–6.

3. Carl J. C. Wolf, *Jonathan Edwards on Evangelism* (Grand Rapids, Mich.: William B. Eerdmans, 1958), ix.

4. William Shakespeare, *Hamlet*.

CHAPTER FIVE

1. Calvin Miller, *Poems of Protest and Faith*.

2. Catherine Marshall, ed., *Mr. Jones, Meet the Master* (New York: Fleming H. Revell, 1958), 145.

3. Calvin Miller, *from my journal*.

CHAPTER SIX

1. William R. Newell, "At Calvary," *The Hymnal for Worship and Celebration* (Waco, Tex.: Word Music, 1986), #338.

CHAPTER SEVEN

1. Musetta Gilman, "Memo to Death," *Trails* (Detroit: Harlo Press, 1986), 58.

2. Quoted in *Religious Quotations* (n.p., n.d.).

3. Benjamin Franklin, cited in Gail & Jill Perry, eds., *A Rumor of Angels* (New York: Ballantine Books, 1989), 151.

4. Edward Chinn, "To Illustrate—Death," *Preaching*, March–April 1991, 56.

5. William Shakespeare, *Hamlet*.

6. Catherine Marshall, ed., *Mr. Jones, Meet the Master* (New York: Fleming H. Revell, 1958), 95.

7. Albert Camus, *The Fall*, trans. Justin O'Brien (New York: Vintage Books, 1956), 11.

CHAPTER EIGHT

1. Cited in Helmut Thielicke, *Christ and the Meaning of Life*, trans. John W. Doberstein (New York: Harper & Row, 1962), 15.

2. John White, *The Race* (Downers Grove, Ill.: InterVarsity Press, 1984), 141.

3. Frederick W. Faber, "Faith of Our Fathers" (1849).

4. Cited in Porter Routh, "How Does God Measure?" *Baptist Program*, November 1963, 10.

5. St. Theresa, cited in St. Alphonsus Liguori, *Love God and Do What You Please!* trans. C. D. McEnniry, ed. M. J. Huber (Liguori, Mo.: Liguori Publications, 1978), 85.

6. Harold Kushner, *When All You've Ever Wanted Isn't Enough* (New York: Pocket Books, 1986), 25.

7. G. K. Chesterton, *"St. Francis of Assisi,"* in *Basic Chesterton* (Springfield, Ill.: Templegate Publishers, 1984), 26.

8. Ibid., 29.

CHAPTER NINE

1. Cited in Arthur C. McGill, *Suffering: A Test of Theological Method*, Paul Ramsey and William F. May, foreword (Philadelphia: The Westminster Press, 1982), 41.

2. Joyce Landorf, *Mourning Song* (Old Tappan, N.J.: Fleming H. Revell, 1974), 155.

3. Cited in Tim Hansel, *When I Relax I Feel Guilty* (Elgin, Ill.: David C. Cook Publishing, 1979), 61–62.

4. *The Catholic Family Book of Novenas* (New York: John J. Crawley, 1956), 2.

5. Helmut Thielicke, *Christ and the Meaning of Life*, trans. John W. Doberstein (New York: Harper & Row, 1962), 15.

6. Cited in Malcolm Muggeridge, *A Third Testament* (New York: Ballantine Books, 1988), 90.

7. Calvin Miller, *from my journal*.

CHAPTER TEN

1. John Updike, "Seven Stanzas at Easter," cited in D. Bruce Lockerbie, *The Liberating Word: Art and the Mystery of the Gospel* (Grand Rapids, Mich.: William B. Eerdmans, 1974), 104–105.

2. Catherine Marshall, ed., *Mr. Jones, Meet the Master* (New York, Fleming H. Revell, 1958), 108.

3. Calvin Miller, *from my journal*.